Advance Praise for

The Epic of You

"Peter shares his story with so much authenticity and grace that it pulls you into a journey of self-examination that's not only about what we accomplish and how we treat others, but more importantly, how we treat ourselves. It's a wonderful blueprint for personal development that allows us to learn from the past and see challenges as gifts that make us who we are. Peter's workbook provides a roadmap for self-discovery that leads to more fulfillment and success at work, home, and in life."

—**Tiffanie Boyd,** global chief people officer,
McDonald's Corporation

"I've known Peter Bailey as a great facilitator, strategist, and leader. This book introduced me to him in an entirely new lens: as a typical human being who endured a radically difficult journey but chose to rise above those circumstances to positively elevate others. Peter courageously shares his life story so we can author a far better story through our lives. Read this book now and thank me later."

—**John O'Leary,** #1 national best-selling author,
On Fire and *In Awe*

"Peter Bailey shares a deeply personal narrative, told with uncommon candor. In doing so, he invites readers to consider their own journey and how the meaning we make of the past can shape what comes next."

—**Scott K. Edinger,** *Wall Street Journal* and *USA Today*
best-selling author, *The Growth Leader*

"This book is one-part true-life adventure story, and one-part life-reframing handbook. It's as if the ghosts of Ernest Hemmingway and Ernest Shackleton teamed up with Brené Brown to help you reinterpret all the changes and disruptions that have led you to where you are today, and reimagine who you can still be tomorrow."

—**Nick Tasler,** best-selling author, *Your Year of Wonders*; contributing writer, *Harvard Business Review*; internationally acclaimed thought leader; organizational psychologist; keynote speaker

"Peter Bailey is hands-down one of the greatest thought-leaders and facilitators in the world. *The Epic of You* reflects his hard-earned experience, reflection, and deep wisdom. As a climbing partner once said, 'growth ain't easy.' Instead, it is a tumultuous process of endings and renewals, death and rebirth. Peter brilliantly reveals this archetypal map that enables us to rip the crust away and live more honestly and heroically, reframing our stories of victimization and tragedy into beauty, power, and purpose."

—**Erik Weihenmayer,** blind adventurer and climber; keynote speaker; cofounder, No Barriers USA; host, *No Barriers Podcast*; author, *Touch the Top of the World*

"Peter Bailey is a mensch: a man of integrity & honor. His book is a real, raw, and relatable heroic journey that is a gift to all who read it."

—**Craig and Patricia Neal,** cofounders, Center for Purposeful Leadership; coauthors, *The Art of Convening*™

"In *The Epic of You*, Peter Bailey is our master guide, illuminating the path to wholeness with great humility and hard-won skill. Using his own full life as a template, like an alchemist he shows us how to turn the raw, sometimes painful stuff of our own lives into the gold of true self. This is a courageous, inevitable journey, for what else is there but to live this one life with as much fullness, gracefulness, and joy as we possibly can?"

—**Henry Emmons, MD,** author, *The Chemistry of Joy* and *The Chemistry of Calm*

"Peter Bailey is like the modern-day Mr. Miyagi—reminding us that we have choices. Those choices are our own to explore, learn from, discard, or enhance. And it's never too late to set a new course or take a ride on ourselves as we authentically follow the guide within."

—**Roshini Rajkumar,** crisis strategist; podcast host, *The Crisis Files*; keynote speaker

"Peter is a true modern-day renaissance man—grounded in integrity, driven to act, and genuinely kind. He lives what he believes, and I admire that."

—**Mark Walinske,** executive director, KidSights™; cofounder and former chairman of the board, CycleHealth; former VP of Innovation and R&D, Optum Health; founder and co-owner, Margo+Lola Fly Fishing School

"As author Peter Bailey so earnestly and rightly puts it, this book is like finding a message in a bottle, one that will throw you a lifeline to save you from drowning in doubts and negativity, float a way of making you the hero of your life story, give you a hold on the true treasure of your experiences, and calm the waves of uncertainty as you move toward an astonishing truth . . . your life is heroic!"

—**Dr. Ronda Beaman,** director of Leadership Studies, Cal Poly State University; chief creative officer, PEAK Learning, Inc.; executive director, DreamMakers SLO; author; executive coach

"To refer to Peter Bailey merely as a consultant is to misrepresent him entirely. He is a wise and empathetic observer of the human condition. His goal—helping people and the organizations they inhabit to become more human—is not only noble, but one he has achieved many times over. In this era of unrest and AI-driven disconnection, *The Epic of You* arrives as a much-needed collection of insights and experiences, filtered through the author's deep wisdom, abiding humanity, and sincere belief that we can become better—and that we must."

—**Peter Himmelman,** Grammy and Emmy nominated singer-songwriter and visual artist; award-winning author, *Let Me Out*; founder, Big Muse

"If you seek peace of soul, or simply to suck the marrow out of the unknown remains of your life, *The Epic of You* is the missing piece. Peter Bailey inspires and guides us to a brighter, happier, more resilient future by reframing and mining the rich ore of our deeply flawed past. Thanks to this book, your heroic journey may have just begun!"

—**Paul G. Stoltz, PhD,** founder and CEO, PEAK Learning, Inc.; author

"Filled with rich storytelling and vulnerability, Peter Bailey nicely reframes his life using the powerful Heroic Journey Mindset. A poet, adventurer, learner, and spiritual advisor, Peter presents a compelling case to reframe certain histories into new, empowering, and transformational narratives. Peter and his book, *The Epic of You*, have improved my life. It's a must-read."

—**Jeff Steinke,** senior vice president of REM & RBS, Ryan Companies US, Inc.

"*The Epic of You* is a generous, gutsy guide for anyone brave enough to ask, 'What now?' If you've ever stood at the edge of possibility wondering, 'Is there more?', you know the complex mix of emotions and obstacles that must be navigated. Peter Bailey helps us do exactly that through his honest, sometimes heartbreaking, and often hilarious exploration of life's pivotal moments. Above all, Peter inspires us to take ownership of our stories—to transform the weight we carry into something powerful that creates real change for ourselves and others."

—**Laura Best,** keynote speaker; author, *Born to Buzz*; founder, Passion Collective.

"This guidebook is more than an epic adventure memoir—it's a mindset map inspired by Peter's remarkable life. It reveals how life's unexpected turns can be reframed from doubt into fuel for growth, purpose, and ongoing self-discovery. If you're ready to turn inward and build a life that's more whole, fulfilling, and meaningful with each passing year, don't just read this book—live it."

—**Tom Wiese,** founder, Wiese Law Firm, Studio/E LLC, ASCENT

"Peter's creativity flows throughout this book. The license plate on his car reads 'CREATE,' and that's how Peter leads his life. If you want to CREATE (or at least explore) the life of your dreams, this book is a must-read."

—**Jeff Prouty,** chairman and founder, The Prouty Project

"Peter Bailey is as real as an author can be. Both insightful and well educated, he combines the lowest points of his history with the zenith of his growth, and what results is this thoroughly engaging work. I was pulled in from the first page and I could see and feel everything he was describing. Highly recommended!"

—**Jeff Dayton,** country songwriter and artist; bandleader, Glen Campbell

"*The Epic of You* is a rare and generous offering—a guidebook for reframing your past and reclaiming your power. Peter charts a course through trauma, addiction, self-doubt, and shame, transforming each into a source of strength, compassion, and purpose. Drawing on Joseph Campbell's *The Hero's Journey,* and his own unforgettable life experiences, Peter invites us to revisit our stories not as victims, but as authors of a life reclaimed. This is a guide forged in fire—full of hard-earned wisdom, shared with care and clarity."

—**Tom Peterson,** publisher, The Creative Company

"The prism of reflection offers understanding and healing that can embolden our future, yet many of us are left in the lowlands with no map. Peter Bailey has captured the essence of this intricate rhythm and generously offers us all the possibility of a new path marked by a compassionate reimagining of ourselves and others with a renewed understanding of our shared humanity and inherent gifts. The poignant writing, penned with humility and grace, about his own adventuresome life twinned with the skill of a world-class facilitator, opens the door with encouragement to bravely explore and integrate the many streams of our own lives."

—**Ann Cahill, MA,** director, The John O'Donohue Legacy Partnership

"Peter Bailey has written a book that is incredibly honest, inspiring, and full of ideas and applications that will help you soar to new heights of the human experience. Be ready, however, to work. *The Epic of You* is for the reader who is willing to explore what it takes to live a life of meaning and fulfillment."

—**David McNally,** CPAE; professional speaker; author, *If You're Alive*; member, Speakers Hall of Fame

"We all carry stories that seem to define us in limiting ways. Peter Bailey's *The Epic of You* is a powerful reminder that we are the authors of our own narratives. Through his unflinching examination of trauma, addiction, and loss, Bailey demonstrates how our most difficult experiences can become our greatest gifts. This book will change how you see your past—and more importantly, how you approach your future."

—**Laura King,** career and alignment strategist; author, *Shine Brighter*

"Peter Bailey, with his brave sharing, authenticity, and courage, invites us to take *The Hero's Journey*. He guides us to be the author and the hero—each of us—of our own wonderful life—whatever age we are. As we all face this time of growing uncertainty and plate-shifting change, Peter is the guide you want. Walk through your heroic journey with one who has taken the path and is living it now—today."

—**David O'Fallon,** former CEO, MacPhail Center for Music; former executive director, Minnesota Humanities Center

"Peter offers a beautifully written, vulnerable, intimate account of two versions of his life. One version is dramas, good and bad, as experienced in the moment, always engaging, and sometimes death-defying. The second is reframed in the narrative of Joseph Campbell's *The Hero's Journey*. This is the guide he would have appreciated when he was a young man trying to make sense of life, and that he continues to use as a mature elder facing new adventures into the unknown. As friends and colleagues, we can attest that Peter embodies the wisdom he offers."

—**William Stockton, PhD & Marjorie Herdes,** copresidents and cofounders, Mobius, Inc.: Partners for Strategic Change

"Peter is an incredibly gifted writer who demonstrates tremendous vulnerability as he guides us through his lifetime of heroic journeys. He provides a clear outline to the reader to help them rewrite the narratives of their lives. Let him become one of your allies to help you navigate your own life challenges."

—**Corey Jensen, DDS,** dentist, Smile Design Dentistry

"In *The Epic of You*, Peter Bailey describes his harrowing path from childhood trauma to a determination to live an examined, whole, and happy life. Peter's courage and honesty in telling his story is a gift to all struggling to find their way out of darkness."

—**Leigh H. Bailey, MA,** CEO and founder, The Bailey Group

THE EPIC OF YOU

REFRAME YOUR PAST TO NAVIGATE YOUR FUTURE

PETER H. BAILEY

GREENLEAF
BOOK GROUP PRESS

This book is intended as a reference volume only. It is sold with the understanding that the publisher and author are not engaged in rendering any professional services. The material presented is for informational purposes and intended for self-discovery and to broaden your horizons, but is not intended for treatment. If you suspect that you have a problem that might require professional treatment or advice, you should seek competent help.

Published by Greenleaf Book Group Press
Austin, Texas
www.gbgpress.com

The "Hero's Journey" graphic was created by Michael Campbell at Radiate Presentation Design.

The "Fire Circle" photograph was taken and granted permission for use by David McClain/CaringBridge.

Distributed by Greenleaf Book Group

For ordering information or special discounts for bulk purchases, please contact Greenleaf Book Group at PO Box 91869, Austin, TX 78709, 512.891.6100.

Design and composition by Greenleaf Book Group and Jonathan Lewis
Cover design by Greenleaf Book Group and Jonathan Lewis
Cover image used under license from ©Adobestock.com/LEEPOWERS

Publisher's Cataloging-in-Publication data is available.

Print ISBN: 979-8-88645-429-1

eBook ISBN: 979-8-88645-430-7

To offset the number of trees consumed in the printing of our books, Greenleaf donates a portion of the proceeds from each printing to the Arbor Day Foundation. Greenleaf Book Group has replaced over 50,000 trees since 2007.

Printed in the United States of America on acid-free paper

25 26 27 28 29 30 31 32 10 9 8 7 6 5 4 3 2 1

First Edition

For Tanya, Sydney, and Jackson,
with so much love and deep gratitude.
You are my world.

Contents

PART FOUR: THE HEROIC JOURNEY GUIDEBOOK

Foreword

In his classic song "Anthem," Leonard Cohen talks about everything in the world having cracks, but that not being a bad thing since it's how the light gets in.

In this book, Peter Bailey "lets the light get in." In the challenging arena of purposeful living and leading, Peter is one of the most accomplished people I know, with the unique capacity to connect role and soul.

But that's not what sets this book apart for me. I find the book eye-opening because Peter does what accomplished people rarely do. He opens his heart and shares his own journey to wholeness. He shows that while everything has imperfections and flaws, those imperfections are what truly let the light get in.

I first met Peter at an Outward Bound Board of Trustees retreat. It was the kind of gathering at which a single question opened the discussion: "Why?" "Why are we here?" I listened quietly as the rotation went around the room. Peter was up before me and when he spoke, he emotionally referred to a very difficult period in his life, one in which "why" had helped him to reframe a narrative in life bigger than himself. By the time Peter finished speaking, he was crying and I was crying, too.

Outside, on the edge of the Boundary Waters Canoe Area wilderness, the granite rock, howling wolves, and frozen lake framed the changing nature of the seasons. Inside, Peter spoke about how he was learning how to reframe his past to navigate his future.

This is a book on that vital role of reframing the narrative in our lives. But, unlike a lot of writing on that topic, it does not begin with a romantic success story. Instead, it begins with Peter's story that opens the pathway into our own challenges and bold endeavors.

None of us escape "the cracks in everything." Peter writes from the spiritual intersection of role and soul to "let the light get in." He explores his insights with elegant simplicity, yet raw courage. He shares, "The heroic journey is a circular path that starts with going on an adventure, confronting challenges, and learning from the hardest parts. We return as changed people."

I felt changed and uplifted after reading this book.

Peter's story and wisdom struck a deep chord within me.

This is a beautiful and timely book that can change your life and might even save it. It will guide you as you travel on your own heroic journey to wholeness.

—Richard Leider, founder of Inventure—The Purpose Company; International best-selling author of *The Power of Purpose*, *Repacking Your Bags*, and *Who Do You Want to Be When You Grow Old?*

Introduction

"Life is not what one lived, but what one remembers
and how one remembers it in order to recount it."
—Gabriel García Márquez, *Living to Tell the Tale*

When asked at a business lunch today why I am writing this book, I paused and thought, while poking at the grilled salmon salad, and then answered: "Because I wanted to write what I wish had been written for me." I have been in the leadership and human performance improvement field for over thirty-five years. I'm the current president of The Prouty Project, a corporate strategic planning and leadership firm. In this role, I have worked with global companies like Medtronic, Ecolab, 3M, McDonald's, General Mills, Mortenson Construction, etc., transforming their teams to be the best version of themselves. I have a Master of Science in Experiential Education, have facilitated hundreds of leadership workshops with thousands of executives, and am a frequent writer in corporate newsletters and on social media. But beyond this and, I believe, more importantly, I am sixty-five years young and have lived a rich and varied life—the best type of "qualification" I have to offer.

I have lived my life as a student of relationships, a collector of books, a novice of multiple musical instruments, a sojourner on the recovery path from addictions, a suburban steward of land and animals, a roaster of Indonesian coffee, a deep-culture global traveler of over fifty countries, and an experimenter of art, dance, and sport—some of which nearly killed me. In some of these pursuits, I have excelled; in many, I have failed. In all, I have been a humble learner.

Oh, and one more thing: I have been and remain a watcher—which means I am cursed with the disease of comparison. Am I doing what I am supposed to be doing? Are they better off than me? Shouldn't I be taller? And what do I do with the challenges I faced growing up, like my father's aneurysm or my mother's alcoholism? What do I do with our loving family's hidden dysfunction and my own battle with PTSD, addictions, and divorces?

At times it has been an arduous journey, growing from a self-centered, fear-based child to a slightly less self-centered, slightly less fear-based adult, picking my way through the minefield of life's challenges with the genuine intention to do no harm, hopefully do some good, and to leave my campsite better than when I found it. I have sometimes handled difficult situations with grace, sometimes kicking and screaming. But rather than continue to be hindered by aspects of my past, I chose to reframe them, seeing them for the gifts that they have been in my life.

We are all experiencing challenging times right now. The world is full of the walking lonely, who wonder what life is all about and why they can't catch a break. Some are recovering from addiction, some are returning from war or living with post-traumatic stress reactions, and some are trying to regain footing after losing their jobs and struggling to find employment late in life. They are the single parents, the twice divorced, the ones with estranged children. They are the millions of amazing people who are living with doubt, fear, and regret, who feel they are the victims of bad choices and missed opportunities. We, myself included, need to rekindle hope and saddle up for the next part of this journey. We need to be stronger in our self-awareness to take on the next set of challenges. And we can't do that from a state of weakness; we can only do that from a position of strength.

I wrote this book for people like me, in need of a new approach, a different way of seeing their pasts as the blueprint of who they are today: unique, wonderful, magical, and gifted. We need to be reminded that all that has happened to us has been a sharpening of our skills for our next great achievement.

While my own life has been a wild roller-coaster ride of both amazing and painful moments . . . overall, I have been more fortunate than not. If asked whether I am ecstatically happy, I would sometimes say, hesitantly, no. Then why not? What is curbing my joy? What is blocking my full celebration of this life? Why am I allowing negative feelings about the things that have happened to me, or any regret over what I did or didn't do, to overshadow the arc of my life?

To pursue that question, I set out to review every memory of my life that cast a negative shadow, to assess and retell it as a positive experience from which I have gained something important that has made me a better person today. By adopting the methodology of Joseph Campbell's Heroic Journey, combined with a mindset of curiosity, courage, and reflection, I embarked on a journey of "wholeness" that changed the story of my life. By doing this work, I learned that lives have a pattern. As a child, I was never taught this and instead flailed, painfully and often ineffectively, believing that I was a failure. This journey to wholeness has given me back the perspective of awe, wonder, and gratitude for the gift of a life that, with the reframing of hindsight, I have been blessed to live. I had to look at some of the painful, diminishing moments and reconcile that even those were of value. Some events I like to say "gave me honey to my heart" and made me more compassionate for the lives and struggles of other people. Some of the painful events actually made me more resilient, and I like to say "gave me strength to my sword arm."

In this book, I offer my own experience, an overview of the Heroic Journey model (upon which I wrote my master's thesis and delivered a TEDx Talk), describe how I reframed my experience using this tool, and share actionable steps one can take to do the same. It is my attempt to roll up what I have learned, stuff it in a bottle, and toss it out to the proverbial seas in hopes it fetches up on a distant shore and into the hands of other fellow wanderers. This reframing has given me the grace and gratitude to take ownership of and have a better appreciation for my life, and I offer it, now, to the world.

PART ONE

A BOLD ENDEAVOR

Chapter One

"As you think, you travel, and as you love, you attract. You are today where your thoughts have brought you; you will be tomorrow where your thoughts take you. You cannot travel within and stand still without."

—JAMES LANE ALLEN

My sister, Pam, and I sat with my mother as she slept the last sleep of her lifetime. She was kept comfortable, and the only indication that she knew we were there was a shift in her breathing when we spoke to her. As my mother lay there, at eighty-three years old, we were unprepared for this transition, since her own mother was in her one hundredth year when she passed. As our mother's adult children, late in life ourselves, we fully expected her to live another seventeen strong years and maybe even crack a hundred.

In hospice, time is an unknown entity. It draws us on like the proverbial ticking mantle clock, minutes, hours, maybe days before the human hourglass of life slips the last trickle of sand through the choke point and all is still. We tried to keep up light conversation with each other, our mother, and the nurses, talking about weather, relatives, and even answering work emails as we hunkered down in our hospice campsite next to her sleeping figure.

The immensity of a passing parent, particularly one's mother, is one we are both still coming to grips with years later. Our father passed away many years ago of a heart attack, alone, and found only the next day at a nursing home in Florida. But sitting here, listening to her gravelly breathing, sighs, and held silence was a different experience.

I offered to fetch dinner, as much to get a break from the closeness and unexpressed emotion as to satisfy hunger. I walked out into the overcast afternoon and across the hospice parking lot with the world going on about itself as worlds do . . . completely unaware of what was happening in our small lives. I ordered cheeseburgers, fries, and Diet Cokes at the McDonald's drive-through. Bruised by the brusqueness of the crackling voice through the speaker, I was shocked by my tenderness. The man on the other side of the speaker didn't know that our mother was dying. He didn't know we would be eating these burgers by her dying bedside. Perhaps I was not ready for the outside world yet, and I scurried back to the room and the safe soft darkness of our time together.

Our mother was dying. The mother who raised us as a mostly single parent. The parent who taught us to ski and play tennis, baked birthday cakes in the shape of flowers and clowns for my sister and Jaguar XKEs for me. The one who took us to the Virgin Islands and across the Middle East to India and Nepal when we were in our teens. Who helped us go to private colleges so that we had the foundation of good educations. Who tried all her life to fill the gap that my father's aneurysm and his life in a nursing home had left. She encouraged us to travel the world as she had throughout her nursing career, and to play chess and read voraciously. She loved the ocean and the beach and taught us to body surf in Maine and Block Island. This was the mother who was now curled in sheets, energy slipping away by the hour.

Memories apparently do flash in front of our eyes as someone dies: images and memories, living videos of conversations, like flipping channels on late-night TV or scrolling Netflix. Scenes of laughter followed by darker-themed plots revealing tense times, tears, and anguish. All of these videos, DVDs, and MP3s make up the Blockbuster Video stores of our lives.

Is that it then? Are our lives a video store of experiences with their separate sections of Comedy, Drama, Romance, and Horror neatly categorized and waiting for our perusal? And which ones define us? Or do they all, the entire catalog, make up our lives? As I sat with my mother and reviewed the videos of memories in my mind, I was struck by the impact her life had had on mine. Many sweet Hallmark moments to cherish to be sure, and yet the others—the ones that seemed to stick out from the shelf—were the painful times, the harsh words, the videos of traumas that I couldn't seem to shake. How was it that I had allowed those memories, those particular video sections, to define me and my sense of self-worth?

This book will challenge the choice I had made up to that point. It will share my realization that by focusing more on the damaging "videos" of my life, I had inadvertently chosen to limit the joy and happiness of all that had happened to and for me. Instead, by reviewing the catalog of my life and owning all of the video sections, I recognized that I could take more ownership of the value that each of these experiences had given me. By reframing them as part of the panoply of my life, I could free myself from the baggage of victimhood and step out onto this later stage of my life—to claim my own life as well lived.

As the son of a disabled Navy pilot and an alcoholic, world-traveling mother who taught us how to live way beyond our means, I was ill-equipped to handle the reality of my life. I sought escapes through alcohol, drugs, sex, and high-risk activities that nearly killed me.

If I remember correctly from college geology classes, there are three kinds of rock—sedimentary, igneous, and metamorphic. Sedimentary is the layering of silt and sand, which then hardens into brittle layers. Igneous is the rock that was once molten, erupted, and then cooled into sharp glass-like obsidian. Metamorphic is rock like granite that changes from time and pressure and heat. Geologically speaking, my hurts and resentments and "little sorrows" were of all three kinds, and they made up the tectonic plates of my life—heavy, grinding, and impenetrable. Deep forces caused by historic embedded events, which played out on the surface of my life every day.

This reframing of my life—in fact, the reframing of all our lives—the naming of geologic events that transpired, is a worthy undertaking. While not for the timid, it is the reframing of who we are in all the aspects of our lives without judgment that brings us to wholeness. It is a self-love process and a re-loving of the people and experiences in our lives that help to heal us.

I embarked on this Heroic Journey to wholeness to change my life. I had been telling my story in a painful, secretive, self-pitying way, and it brought a certain limited set of behaviors. I have found that by simply owning everything that happened to me in a different way, even the hard stuff makes more sense. The challenges were part of my training. The loneliness and depressions were because I was overriding or ignoring something more important. When I got out of feeling sorry for myself and looked around, I realized I was actually able to improve my life, and maybe that experience could help someone else.

Joseph Campbell speaks about the Heroic Journey being a process where something has to die for a new thing to be born. The "me" I thought I knew needed to die so that I could become the "me" who was more evolved. I had to let go of my old, limited story so that I could live a better, healthier, more abundant life.

Chapter Two

"Maybe there is no fresh wisdom, just old woes,
new words to name them by, and the will to act."

—AMANDA GORMAN

Changing the narrative of one's life is a bold endeavor. Immediately, alarm bells may go off for some people whose truly horrible life incidents have seemingly no redeeming qualities. I am certainly not claiming that the Holocaust, the murder of family members, or the 9/11 attacks, for example, were "good things." I can only report from my own experience, and I found that combing through the history of my life, searching for key moments of blame, victimization, abuse, and hardship, allowed me to reframe what has happened to me as exactly as they were supposed to be for my journey of discovery. Told differently, those events became rites of passage, trials by fire, dark nights of the soul, and hard times in the crucible, which made me who I am today. From reframing the stories of my life, I now better appreciate all that has happened—not just the dolphin and butterfly moments but the whole ball of sticky wax, so I can walk more fulfilled into a future, knowing now that my life was well lived.

One might argue that this isn't important or possible. Yet it's helpful to consider all the times each day we send ourselves negative messages that confine us to our pasts instead of assuring us that our strengths are hard earned.

Joseph Campbell, the historian, philosopher, and college professor, delved into human life stories as a modern mythology, a source of our archetypes and patterns, which seem to be woven through the fabric of every culture around the world across the ages.

I will articulate the stages he defined later, but for now, in its simplest form, the Heroic Journey is a circular path that starts with going on an adventure, confronting challenges, and learning things from the hardest parts. We then return as changed people, often to communities and families who can't appreciate or understand what we have been through. Returning veterans, cancer survivors, and those recently divorced are common and obvious examples—people trying to regain their footing with families and coworkers after experiencing untold traumas that have changed them forever.

I did my graduate thesis on the Heroic Journey and delivered a TedX Talk on "Developing your Heroic Journey Mindset" as a way to continually remind myself to practice seeing the Heroic Journey in our lives. I see the Heroic Journey circle as an illumination of stages and events that are hopeful, and by naming the Journey, I can better understand it. If I can better understand it, then I will more likely learn from it. My hope is that you, too, will better understand the journey you have been on and the choices you have made and will stand taller for the accomplishment and richness you are bringing forward from your experiences.

PART TWO

MY STORY, AS I TOLD IT

Chapter Three

"Pain, pleasure, and death are no more than a process for existence. The revolutionary struggle in this process is a doorway open to intelligence."

—FRIDA KAHLO

When my mother was still pregnant with me, my father, a former Navy pilot, suffered a sudden brain hemorrhage, an aneurysm. In the late 1950s, this wasn't as common as it is today, and the treatment was barbaric. To stop the bleeding, they removed large parts of his cerebellum, impacting his speech, which would be slurred forever, and destroying his balance, hampering his ability to walk unassisted ever again.

Somehow my father survived the surgery and later came home to stay with us. My mother worked multiple shifts as a registered nurse and tried to also manage his caregiving, in the early 1960s, despite his mood swings, depression, unintelligible speech, and explosive anger. She had my sister a year and a half later, because she always wanted two children. "Your sister, Pam, is my gift to you," she would tell me often.

I was born in December of 1959 and came into this world and this family with a feeling that something was very wrong, and I was somehow responsible for the stress I felt in our second-floor apartment. I remember looking out the window when I was five and too young to be out with the older children playing in the evening light. The laughter of kids chasing each other made me feel so alone. The silence of the apartment was deafening. Where were the adults, I wonder now? Where was my sister? I can't seem to remember anything but the lonely, quiet apartment and the heaviness of the air. The one bright spot I had was my window ledge where my mother had sprinkled grass seed on cotton in an aluminum oven-broiler tray. Every day I would go to the window and see how much the sprigs of grass had grown while I was at school.

[The author at age five.]

Each day I would walk to school, past the apartments and the long row of garages. And each day I would come home for lunch and then go back for the afternoon of first grade. One day, my mother had to stay at the hospital and had called the principal of the school, a friend of the family, to urgently request that he keep me at school because she could not come home that day. He forgot to tell me, and I walked home as usual, mounted the stairs, and knocked on the door for my mother. There was no answer. I waited and knocked again. I had to pee. She had never not been home for my lunchtime. I reached under the small wooden stool where we kept the key, but there was no key this time. As a five-year old, waiting outside the door, my mind raced to the worst possible scenario, and I believed the only reason she wouldn't open the door was because she was dead inside the apartment. I started to cry, and then, sobbing on the wooden stool, I couldn't hold back the pee anymore, and I soaked the floor, pee spreading into the wiry, brown doormat.

My sobs grew louder as I called for my mother, pounding on the door. The neighbor downstairs eventually heard me and came up to take me in. She cleaned me up and gave me lunch. She told me my mother was probably held up at the hospital and would be home soon. Perhaps, but the seeds of doubt, fear, and betrayal were planted like grass in cotton. No matter what happened, I anticipated the worst. Fear governed me and grew around my heart like vines choking me tighter and tighter.

When I was in third grade, we moved from the apartments to another part of town in North White Plains, to a little white salt-box house on a tree-lined street across from a highway. My mother worked two jobs, and my father was in a nursing home. To fill the gap from lack of adult attention and to numb the feelings of free-floating anxiety, I became a class clown. I acted out in class, doing anything to get a laugh, and took risks to improve my position in my peer group. At George Washington Elementary School, I climbed an eighty-foot chimney crack in the back of the school gymnasium many times to collect the gym balls that were stuck there.

I'd wedge my back against the brick wall and then pull both feet up against the other side. Then I'd push up, moving my back up, moving one foot up at a time, nothing to hold onto, only the pressure from my legs and back keeping me in this three-foot chimney. I'd smile, thinking *This is easy*, but as I'd get higher, I'd begin to sweat and my legs would begin to shake. Forty feet. Now eighty feet. It was horribly dangerous, but it won me praise, and I lived on praise.

The term at the time for my friends and I, who often roamed the tree-lined neighborhoods on our own with no adult supervision, was "latchkey kids." As I think back on those times, I remember my friends, but I can't picture any of their parents. They were always either at work or fighting in kitchens, and we rarely saw them. On the positive side, it gave us room to be adventurous and inventive. Anything and everything became a game of challenge. As dangerous as train tracks were, they provided hours of entertainment. We would walk them, balancing for as long as we could, or flatten coins into copper and silver leaves. We would invent competitions that tested our strength and bravery. One time, we found a corrugated water drainage pipe about eighteen inches wide that ran underneath the railroad tracks to drain water from one side of the hill to the other side of the tracks. It was full of rubble, inches of water, and skittering rats. We found that if you wormed your way into it just as the trains passed over, the shaking of the earth and the roar of the train felt like the world was coming to an end. This both thrilled and terrified us—again, a chance to feel something other than sad or numb, to feel alive.

Elementary and middle school days were spent riding bikes, climbing trees, smoking Newport cigarettes, and getting dizzy and falling from the branches. We watched Evel Knievel movies over and over and then jumped our bikes over ramps and cliffs trying to be like him.

Jack Wild played the Artful Dodger in the musical *Oliver!*, and he became one of my heroes. I took up shoplifting like him for a short time (until a friend got caught), and I began to adopt a mock-British accent. There was a newspaper and candy store on the way to school that stacked *Playboy* and *Penthouse* magazines in front of the counter. We found that if you put your notebooks down on the stack, paid for your candy, and then picked up your notebooks, you could get away with a magazine or two every time.

We were unsupervised and wild, seeking adventure, seeking something to fill us with purpose and adrenaline, challenging each other to greater and greater feats of adolescent machismo. One of the most terrifying dares involved me and a two-hundred-foot bridge over a six-lane freeway outside of the city of White Plains on my walking route to school.

"Chicken!" Johnny and David yelled at me up on the bridge.

Traffic rushed a hundred feet below me as I clung to the outside of the chain-link fence over the highway. Each grip shifted me sideways across the outside the bridge. I moved my right hand and then moved my right sneaker, twisting my Keds into the square fence hole. Moved my left hand and then moved my left foot. Told myself to breathe and to not look down.

I remember being over the center of the bridge and not being able to look down. The gray galvanized fence stretched tight across the center of the bridge . . . I kept on moving. Reached my hand right, then stepped right. My hands sweated as I heard cars honking, as they saw me above them as they sped by. When I was at the highest point of the bridge, I couldn't feel my fingers as they gripped the steel fence . . . I begged them to stay closed like a claw. Johnny and David were quiet as they watched. I had to show them I wasn't chicken. Had to prove it to myself. I released my feet and dangled them over the road. I pulled myself back up, my breathing out of control. I jabbed a toehold and moved right, had to keep moving. I saw the end of the bridge still so far away. I felt my numb fingers begin to lose grip. I talked to my hands, told them to hold on. I wiped a smeared tear off my face, begged my sneakers to please hold. My back and neck were killing me. My fingers had stopped listening, had grown numb. I pictured the claws of an eagle that opened and closed on the fence, each claw circling the thin metal and closing like a ring. More cars honked, traffic slowed down . . . I couldn't look down, but I knew down was down there. I saw the far edge of the bridge closer than before. I moved my feet. I moved my claws. My right sneaker got stuck, wouldn't come out. I wrenched at it again as I clung to the fence, each step closer to the end of the bridge. I drifted away and looked at myself on the bridge. I looked like a GI Joe doll. Watched as I moved across and up to the railing. Another twenty feet and I made it, but I couldn't feel my hands. They were grubby, bloody, and chafed. I gasped for air as Johnny and David caught up to me.

"Can't believe you did that! That was so stupid!"

I was thirteen years old. I slung my backpack over my shoulder, my hands like someone else's. I walked behind them the rest of the way to my seventh-grade class at Eastview Junior High School.

My father lived with us for six years after the surgery, but whatever they did to him made him a completely different person. He would get angry about nothing. Raise his voice and get frustrated when we asked him to repeat himself because we couldn't understand what he was saying. Or he would lie on the couch silent and sullen for days. After six years, my mother realized she couldn't raise two kids and take care of this man. My mother made a difficult decision and put him into a nursing home and filed for a divorce. My father's Catholic family never forgave her for that and excommunicated her from the family with whom she had grown so close.

After some time, she made an attempt at a second marriage, but that deteriorated into loud verbal fighting. In a small home, the stress became unbearable. Pillows over my head at night blocked out some of the yelling as I cried myself to sleep. During that time, it was painfully obvious that I was failing fifth, then sixth, and then seventh grade; if it wasn't for Miss Petty, my English teacher, I would never have passed a class. She taught humanities, and we read and wrote poetry. I began writing what I was feeling. She was a kind and dedicated teacher, and she said she saw something in me.

Each walk home from school was a serpentine trail through a minefield, picking streets to avoid fights or shakedowns for money. Nights were spent curled in bed, overhearing the fighting between my mother and stepfather. My escapes were stolen *Playboy* and *Penthouse* magazines stacked under the bed, and I would draw pictures of myself as a child with no mouth, no way to speak out. I would scribble crayon pictures of my mother and stepfather and tape them to the door: "Hate you both." A twitch developed, shaking the long hair out of my eyes, even when it wasn't in my eyes. I bit my nails and worried about everything. A seventh-grade yearbook entry from another kid said: "See you next year, Twitch."

I dreaded each day, walking to school in fear and unworthiness and living in loneliness. Nightmares woke me most nights, and each nail-biting day was consumed with worries about everything.

This was my life as a child, though my sister Pam's experience varied widely from my own. As Elisa Bernick says in her powerful memoir, *Departure Stories*, "Memory is a slippery fish."[1] Connected to my mother and father in her own way, Pam did not exhibit the same codependent tendencies. Where I lived with the heightened sensitivities and self-doubt of one destined for addictions, she leaned more toward the logical and the practical, and while there has always been a deep love for her as my sister, our approaches to life were vastly different and cut a path of distance between us, then and now.

---

1 Elisa Bernick, *Departure Stories: Betty Crocker Made Matzoh Balls (and Other Lies)* (Indiana University Press, 2022).

I wasn't always alone, but I felt like I was. The self-conscious thoughts and voices in my head were my world. The loss of my father due to his injury and the absence of my hard-working mother left me trying to put together the path for my life with puzzle pieces that didn't fit, that were parts of other people's puzzles. I couldn't see what my picture was supposed to be. I had no idea how to live my life.

Chapter Four

"We make the world we are living in. And we have to make it over."

—JAMES BALDWIN

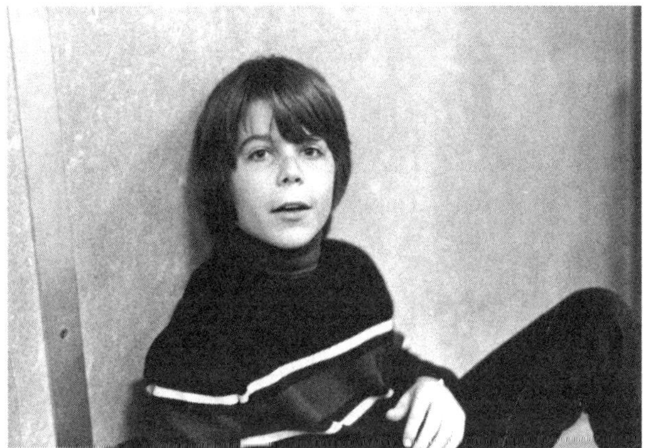

[The author in seventh grade at The Harvey School, Katonah, New York.]

To get me out of the suburban distraction of shoplifting, smoking cigarettes, and cutting classes, my mother moved us from the little white house in White Plains closer to where she taught high school in the affluent town of Chappaqua, in Northern

Westchester County. She was done with her second marriage, and their divorce was settled quietly, almost like it didn't happen. From the cracker box–sized white house, we now had a sprawling, barn-red fixer-upper home set back on a long driveway in Bedford Village. This was another world—a completely different type of adventure.

Instead of a lawn, we had woods, a swamp, and a meadow over the hill. The swamp had treasures like skunk cabbage and mud holes I called quicksand. The meadow had hawks, crows, blue jays, and black snakes. I read a book about a boy who ran away to a hollow tree and trained a peregrine falcon. He lived as a part of nature, not apart from it, and I wanted to be him, making a fort in the tops of trees and talking to birds and squirrels. As opposed to the harmful ways I sometimes tried to escape, nature offered me actual healing, and I started a lifelong love for it here.

Given an air rifle, I shot at paper targets and cans until one day, I hit a chickadee and grieved the tenderness of the life I had just taken. Life was precious, I realized. Living things mattered. I cried inconsolably.

My mother must have forgotten this when she asked me to kill the kittens.

"We have too many kittens!" she said one morning, as she got dressed and brushed her teeth. "Please drown them in the toilet."

I didn't know what to say or do. I wanted to please my mother, but I loved those kittens.

I held the first tiny, squirming body underwater: the black one, her little paws splaying as she paddled trying to break free from my grip. The kitten took a long time to die. Then the white, speckled one, and then the orange-and-white one. Some of the kittens were in Ziplock baggies full of water, but there was an air bubble. I submerged all eight kittens while my mother finished her coffee and raced to get ready for work in her underwear.

Something inside me broke. My chest cracked open, and my heart became bigger than my rib cage, making me feel everything more than the average bear. Reluctantly, I'd done as she'd asked—the first time I vividly remember doing so but certainly not the last. The bigger house and property meant more work and chores to keep it up. While beautiful, it came with the stress of having to shovel the long driveway in winter, repair where the carpenter ants ate into the outside wall, and paint the exterior house walls and trim.

One night when I was thirteen, around two a.m., I tiptoed up to the apartment we were renting out over the garage, and I painted all the stairs as a surprise for my mother so that she wouldn't have to. We were a small family, and she needed more help than my sister and I could deliver. I took it upon myself as the "man of the house" and painted all the stairs with the brown paint she wanted, in the dark, keeping quiet so I didn't wake her. I was eager to show her what I did the next morning, but her depression lingered on, and she didn't show any reaction to what I had done on her behalf.

I wanted to be enough or do enough to warrant the praise she sometimes gave. Like a slot machine in Vegas, she paid out erratically, and the more she wavered, the harder I tried to appease the volatile being her alcoholism created. Maybe this time. Maybe the next. I attempted to read the signs in the fog of depression that hung over our home. The silence. The anticipation of a blowup. After one particularly bad night, she smashed her glass of scotch on the tile kitchen floor in a rage about something and stormed off to bed. I dutifully cleaned all the broken glass up so our dog wouldn't cut her paws. I would phone home and listen to the nuances of her voice to see if she was happy or in one of her depressions or had been drinking. If I could just pull the handle of the family slot machine a few more times, we might all win.

Life in our single-parent alcoholic home was a confusion of love and laughter followed by depression and silence. We would experience the good life of ski trips and beach holidays and then suffer through stressful money talks and my mother's periodic crying jags. We lived beyond our means and then somehow scraped it together so we had enough money. We seemed to have nothing, and we seemed to have everything. I was crippled by low self-esteem, self-doubt, and fear of what might happen next.

I lived this way in every relationship I had from then on. I had no power except my ability to "read the air" and interpret what might be the right thing to say or do. I couldn't tell you what my favorite color was; it's whatever yours is. "Blue? Yeah, me too."

Though I was already in seventh grade when we moved, I was made to repeat it, so I could catch up with the rest of my class. I received a partial scholarship at The Harvey School, at that time still a private all-boy's school in the neighboring town of Katonah. They required us to wear a jacket and tie, study Latin and Greek, attend an hour of study hall, and play three hours of mandatory sports every day. I entered the world of the well-to-do and lapsed into the old habit of speaking with a British accent. Fellow students were a mix of famous families with seven chimneys on their homes and scholarship kids from New York City. I didn't know where I fit in.

Life was lived through other people. The disease of comparison ruled me. My clothes were always just a little off. I was either painfully underdressed or inappropriately overdressed, a dead giveaway that I didn't belong. I was a spy, always on the verge of being caught and humiliated. I thought if only I could talk the language of brands and experiences, I might bolster how I came across and have more value in my peers' eyes.

Due to my mother's ability to manifest experiences beyond our means, I was often able to pony up with the currency of conversation. "Yes, I have traveled across Asia." "Yes, I have sailed in the Caribbean and lived for a summer on a private cove on St. John in the US Virgin Islands." "Yes, I have Rossignol F5 skis"—the best you could buy at the time (because my mother worked at an upscale ski shop as a second job). I wanted to be a rich man's son, and my mother worked hard to make me look like one. But it was hollow. I was painfully alone. The masquerade worked for only a short time. Nothing I said made me equal to them in my eyes. Nightmares haunted me most nights. Comparison, low self-esteem, and shame—about being a poorer kid at a private school and because of the erratic behavior from my only parent at home—all contributed to these dark days.

One time, on the walk home from seventh grade, my friends and I snuck into the cemetery with my friend Billy's sister. She was older, and she would let us touch her.

"It's my job to teach you boys how to kiss," she said.

One by one, we would go up behind a stone mausoleum and she would show us how to open our mouths just right, and how to use our tongues.

When it was my turn, I climbed the slight hill and saw her sitting cross-legged, her back against the stone. She smiled and looked beautiful, despite her grubby, pink sweater. No girl had ever smiled at me like that.

"Hey," she said, "come sit here next to me."

She sat me on her coat and leaned toward me. She put her hand on the side of my face, and I smelled her shampoo mixed with cigarettes as I got closer. She said to close my eyes and open my mouth part way but not all the way. As she inched closer, I went electric. Her mouth pressed mine, and I could feel every cell in my body arc at the same time. Her mouth opened, a vast softness as her lips parted and her tongue slid into my mouth.

"It's okay," she said. "Push your tongue forward a little bit . . . but not too much."

I was woozy and alive. I drifted away in an affectionate blur that made my face blend into hers. My entire consciousness was alive, my whole being and world focused on the sensations of my tongue and mouth swelling to encompass my life and every moment that had led up to that moment. The sunlight flickering through the maple leaves above us looked like the light of a cathedral. She was an angel, and I was flying.

"Mmm, you taste good, like cinnamon," she said.

I knew two things from that moment on: I wanted to get really good at kissing, and I would chew cinnamon gum for the rest of my life.

Drinking started at thirteen too, in the back of the school at a dance, with a bottle of Boone's Farm Strawberry Hill. After my friends and I split a bottle, my world changed. I was funnier. The girls looked prettier, and I thought French kissing was more likely to happen. The pursuit began for more of whatever was in that bottle and the next female who would let me kiss her. All my troubles seemed to drop away, and I found a new escape.

After wading through the murky, confusing world of my earlier years, unsure about everything, things had now become clear: I wanted to drink and I wanted to have sex. At fifteen, I had sex for the first time in the basement guest bedroom with the sixteen-year-old sister of family friends, on her insistence. It was a disaster. Her father discovered us and chased us out, but my world rocked again. I began to obsess about having relationships. Over the course of my life, everyone I met was a possible relationship.

As a people watcher, I was captivated by how people lived their lives. Did they touch? Did they look happy together? How did they treat other people? I learned how to interact by watching other people interact. I fell in love with people.

This sensitivity to others—their moods, their wishes and desires, their behavior as a tool for learning how to move in the world—helped me become adept at people-pleasing, a coping mechanism that would later help me navigate my working world but would haunt my personal relationships. I had an insatiable need for love, and I would go to great lengths to find it. From that first kiss in the cemetery, I searched the world for that feeling again and again.

Chapter Five

"You cannot run away from a weakness; you must sometimes fight it out or perish. And if that be so, why not now, and where you stand?"

—ROBERT LOUIS STEVENSON

By the time I entered high school, I was a codependent, lonely, self-conscious mess. I was a new kid in the ninth grade at Horace Greeley High School in Chappaqua. I lived miles away, in Bedford Village. At sixteen, I didn't drive yet, and I was dependent on my mother for rides to and from school every day. I didn't grow up with my classmates, who had all been through the feeder middle school together. Long before drones were invented, I felt that I was witnessing my life as if a camera were watching me at all times through everything I did: carrying my lunch tray to a table. Walking to my locker. This hyper-self-consciousness was relentless and added to my sense of separation. I could see my life as it was happening to me. I was an actor in a B movie, and it wasn't going well.

While never the best athlete in high school, I loved sports and played soccer in the fall, played tennis and lacrosse in the spring, and wrestled and skied in the winters. Many of my punishing athletic sessions were followed up by a typical, even more painful family scenario, like this day following a wrestling practice.

A fellow high school wrestler lifted me off my feet and slammed me down, smearing a Nike swoosh of sweat on the mat with my face. I twisted to break his grip. A blur of guys stood around me in a circle yelling. The guy was way stronger, and he slammed me down again. I tried to get up. Attempted a reversal. With one arm around my neck, he hooked my knee, driving me toward a cradle pin, stacking me upside down as I struggled. During wrestling practice, "Shark Bait" was the dreaded challenge, which pitted six guys against one, one after another, to help us develop endurance. A whistle echoed in the gym, and he jumped off me and tagged another guy in for the next two-minute rotation. A final whistle sounded, and I was done. Thank you, Jesus. Nothing left of me but hamburger meat.

At the end of the night, we would roll up the rubber mats and drag them against the wall before we hit the showers. The locker room would echo like a prison when the steel locker doors slammed. All of us would clamber out to parents waiting in a cold line of headlights, which would light up the steam clouds coming from our breath and bodies. I would look for my mother's car. She drove a 1974 Ford Gran Torino Squire station wagon, tan with wood siding and a hood as long as a Ping-Pong table. Cars would come and go, but I wouldn't see her. Geno, the custodian, would sweep the halls with a double-wide push broom, like a dust Zamboni, making long passes down the corridor before he picked up each pile at the end of the hall. To kill time and look like I didn't care, I would read the announcements on the bulletin board by the apple vending machine: posters of upcoming student elections, a choir concert, a bike for sale. All the others would be gone and I would still be waiting, the last one—again.

The Klieg lights in the main gym would switch off, the electric buzz now silent. I'd wait by the glass sports trophy case, with the gray team photos, in the hall by the front doors. Geno would look for things to do. "You have a ride coming?" he would ask.

"Yes, but we live in Bedford Village, and it takes my mom awhile to get here."

He would nod and wipe fingerprints off the glass doors. He would wander off and then come back. "I have to close up the building," he would say reluctantly.

"Ok," I'd say. The indoor lights would switch off. It was winter and it was cold, and my breath would hang like a haint in the spotlight. The parking lot would be completely empty. Geno's old blue Chevelle would chug up the hill and away into the night.

My mother worked as the school nurse at the high school, but we lived in another town, and after driving home at the end of a day, she might have a glass of wine or two, or maybe a scotch. Things would slow down, and she could lose track of time. I would zip up my coat and tug my hat lower. She was probably tired and taking a break before making the forty-five minute drive back to get me. My sister, Pam, would have been home by then, and they might have gotten involved in something. Wrestling practice was from three to six p.m. every day through the winter, and she would have to come back every day to get me.

Waiting to be picked up firmly pressed the "unworthiness" button in me (if I was deemed of value, she would have shown up on time), and this contributed to my inordinate relationship with time in later years. I swore I would never make someone else wait for me, never let them feel what I felt after wrestling practice.

Then one day, my mother came home from work with a question:

"Hey, kids . . . want to drive to India?"

It was *worded* as a question, but in my mother's exuberant way, it meant we were going. She had seen an ad in *The New York Times* for a group bus trip from Germany to Nepal over ten weeks for only $333 per person. It was 1976, and the hippie trail to Kathmandu was in full swing. So the summer of my sophomore year of high school, instead of being bored at home or working a summer job, my sister, mother, and I traveled through Germany, Austria, Yugoslavia and Bulgaria, Turkey, Iran, Afghanistan, Pakistan, India, and Nepal in a blunt-nosed Mercedes bus with twelve other overlanders bound for adventure across Central Asia to the Himalayas. I had no idea what adventures lay ahead, but I was ecstatic. We were signing on for a trip from Frankfurt, Germany, to Kathmandu, Nepal; ten weeks and all that was being provided was the seat on the bus and suggestions on places to stay when we got to the various cities. Our time was spent mostly staring out the wide windows at the myriad of sights and sounds of Central Asia. Our fellow travelers were a mixed bag of a New York City waiter, a psychiatrist, two medical students, an advertising executive, an heiress from Connecticut, and another single-mother family with two daughters about my sister's and my age.

Jan, our group leader, was an art collector and rumored to be Lenny Bruce's former secretary. She would drop us off at a flea-bitten hotel or youth hostel and yell out the window, "Meet me on this corner tomorrow morning at seven a.m. or catch up to the bus in the next town." She meant it, and we never missed the bus. We suspected she was smuggling art and cultural artifacts in the underbelly of the bus and using tourists as a cover. She carried a pistol with one bullet in it and told us, "If I am ever surrounded by nomadic tribesmen eyeing me with ill intent, the bullet is for me."

Part way through the trip, we stayed at the majestic Shah Abbas Hotel (now the Abbasi Hotel) in Isfahan, Iran. It was an exquisite three-hundred-year-old heritage site, then managed by Intercontinental Hotels, with enclosed gardens, bubbling fountains, and strolling peacocks. Lazy days were spent lolling on pillows by the fountains, smoking snake-long hookah pipes, and sipping sweet tea. Marcella, a young woman in the group, and I had run up the foothills of Mount Ararat in Turkey and gotten sick from heat prostration, with muscle cramps, chills, and fevers the week before. I had recovered, but Marcella had had enough of the trip and wanted to go back to Connecticut. I accompanied her up to Tehran on a crowded bus, five hours over 250 miles to the airport, where we spent the night waiting for her flight. After we said our goodbyes, I made my way downtown to a hotel when the city of Tehran suddenly erupted into riots. What seemed like an easy trip to the airport had taken a dangerous turn.

People ran down the streets and in and out of buildings, yelling to each other. They flipped cars over and lit them on fire. I didn't know what was going on or which way to run, and I didn't know who to ask. I took shelter in a dingy hotel, where they gave me a filthy room with filthy brown sheets. I was hungry and had no food. I peered from my second-floor window at the violence and mayhem. I saw a newsstand halfway down the block, where I thought I could get something to eat. I left the safety of the hotel and crouched low as I ran down to the corner. I bought three bottles of water and two packs of crackers and raced back. I jolted at the sound of an explosion and dropped one of the bottles and kept on running. The hotel clerk followed me up to my room, where I discovered my door didn't lock. He leered at me and asked if there was anything I wanted, anything at all. He wouldn't leave. He looked at me for a long time before he finally left. I moved the only chair and table to block the door. The yelling in the streets, fires, and exploding cars continued all night.

The next morning dawned with an eerie quiet. I picked my way through the rubble in the streets of Tehran to the bus station and somehow got on the right bus back to Isfahan.

When I think back on this event, I am struck by the inconceivable fact that I was alone at sixteen in a riotous city and able to navigate my way through danger. I still get PTSD flashbacks when I smell diesel fuel or am in situations where there is yelling and chaos.

Although a mediocre student in high school, I easily learned Turkish and Farsi to bargain in the marketplaces. Sleight-of-hand coin tricks and pantomime entertained the kids who playfully followed us. I was in love with this world: bells on camels and horse wagons creating the movie montage soundtrack across the Middle East; the smell of roasting corncobs on curbside brazier grills; the steam of Turkish baths in Istanbul, with the marble steps rounded by a thousand years of wooden sandals; the Grand Bazaar, with its hanging carpets, goat-skin coats, and mirrored mosaic tapestries; the pointed-roof caves of Cappadocia standing like dribble castles in the desert, with grotto paintings of Christian frescoes by eleventh-century monks; bargaining for turquoise jewels in Meshad, Iran; riding horses in the escarpment in Bamyan and Band-e Amir, Afghanistan; the blur of color, sights, sounds, smoke, and smells that is India. I was comfortable in this world. I was home. I loved the traveling, the people, the sky, the endless vistas, and my inner Mowgli danced.

Ray, my roommate on the trip to Nepal, was a New York psychiatrist who introduced me to hashish. We smoked every night and laughed hysterically about the rooms, the people on our trip, and the way he folded his crisp shirts in baggies every day for ten weeks. Think of a stoned Felix Unger. I was learning about life in a whole new classroom.

We smoked hash all the way across Turkey and Iran and Afghanistan. However, a sign at the border between Afghanistan and Pakistan cautioned:

"Hashish is legal in Afghanistan, but if Pakistanis catch you, may Allah help you."

Becky, one of the women on the trip, and I discussed what we should do with our chunks of hashish we had that were the size of our thumbs. She had one too . . . We looked at each other and with sheepish smiles decided to eat them. Perhaps that was unwise.

Blurry photographs of people and places reveal a period of four days in Northern Pakistan that I barely remember. Raised thresholds and low doorways posed a problem for my clouded mind and were hard for me to navigate. I don't know the number of face-plants I made that week, but it was way too many.

When I returned home months later, my doctor attributed me having the first documented case of giardiasis in Westchester County to that little eating fiasco.

In Band-e Amir, Afghanistan, my fifteen-year-old sister and I traded wool socks to a shepherd so we could rent his two horses and ride them into the desert. It was cold, and we left the tent camp and headed along a thinly marked trail in the rock and sand. Pam was not feeling well, and we did not know that the 8,700-foot elevation might be causing her altitude sickness. Band-e Amir was a remarkable oasis of lakes, with mineral water that seeped and poured over the cliffs. In 2009, it became the first national park in Afghanistan, but this was 1976, and no one knew we were there. Our horses started to gallop toward the edge of the cliffs; we could barely keep them reined in. They knew these trails well, and yet we were in constant danger of being tossed over the cliffs. We were alone in the fading light, rock, sand, sky, and endless Afghanistan horizon. We returned to camp just before darkness fell. Pam was really sick now, with chills and a bad headache. Our mother had no idea. She was back in Kabul, 150 miles and five hours of travel away, canoodling with a Canadian professor teaching at the University of Kabul. We shivered under yak wool blankets in a yurt in the bleak expanse of the high mountain desert of Northern Afghanistan—another occasion where we were left alone in a potentially dangerous situation to fend for ourselves. We grew from experiences like these, but not without emotional costs.

Volumes have been written about India, and more can still be told about the myriad of sights, sounds, and smells. For me, entering the Punjab during monsoon season meant living in a gray-palette watercolor, flooded roads, cows in knee-deep water, and the only respite being the dairy bars, which served chocolate-pineapple-flavored water buffalo milk in misshapen blue-glass bottles. Windshield wipers on the bus swiped at rain but couldn't keep up with the downpour. Most of our luggage was kept on top of the roof, and the water found its way into everything. Sadly, the Turkish embroidered goat-skin coat that I had bargained for in German with the Turkish shop owner in the Istanbul Grand Bazaar, destined for my high school girlfriend Linda, had become a sopping heavy sponge smelling more goaty than when the goat was alive. It was reluctantly jettisoned before it drew flies.

[Man on street in Jaipur—1976.]

We traveled throughout India, taking on the classic sites of the Red Fort and the Taj Mahal, the Pink City of Jaipur, and then on to

Varanasi to see the burning ghats on the river's edge of the Ganges, before heading back north and up to Gorakhpur and into Nepal.

I was not prepared for the smell of human bodies being burned on funeral pyres. The acrid smoke caught in the back of my throat and made me retch. The dead bodies' last grasp on us before they danced on smoke up to the heavens. Quiet mourning families raked remains of unburnt bones into the river and cleaned up the cement pads for the next grieving families who waited for their turn. Worshippers waded and practiced ablutions in the muddy current as the stream of floating coals and a dead cow drifted swiftly by. The power of Spirit reigned in India. Monks meditated on traffic medians amid the maya of mayhem. Sports cars slunk past twisted-limbed children who begged for rupees on curbsides. Contemplative compassion overlayed smoldering racial tensions. Protected heavy-lidded sacred cows jammed streets, oblivious to traffic. Bent car wheel rims were hammered like armor to fight potholes another day. A cacophony of car repair shops banged away—a symphony of the city tuning up their instruments for another day.

My personal definition for *adventure* has long been "the juxtaposition of the incongruous and the commonplace." India captures that juxtaposition completely, and it was starting to reveal to me the adventure that was my life. Having sex at an early age and exposure to the myriad of humankind in its beauty and it's rawness burned me indelibly to my core. I call those horrible or exquisite experiences that touch me and leave an indelible mark *lifeburns*. How could I make sense of human depravity, violence, and hate at sixteen? How could I account for the cruelty to animals and twisted-limbed begging children next to the grandeur of witnessing the majestic marble of the Taj Mahal under the glow of a full moon? I wondered this, as I walked the path beside the reflecting pool of the Taj Mahal, captivated by the illumination of the dome and minarets in the full moon night.

Suddenly I slipped and fell into the long, shallow fountain pool. I came up spitting and soaking wet, a baptism into the murky waters of life, the reflection of all that is holy, human, ethereal, and earthy. Life is an immersive experience, and I was dripping wet.

The road trip across the globe from Frankfurt, Germany, to Katmandu, Nepal, was a liberal arts education in global cultures, linguistics, world economies, and environmental impact. I emerged from the ten-week trip a different being than when I began. I coined the term *lifeburn* for experiences that seared deep into my soul and psyche, burning into me a primal tattoo of love for life as well as a wariness for the evil that lurks below the surface of humanity and an undying belief in the good, the love, and the godliness of the art and spirituality of life. I was a novitiate, a pilgrim walking the first stretch of my lifeline with awarenesses revealed that would carry me into the next phase of my journey.

Chapter Six

"Africa has her mysteries, and even a wise man cannot understand them. But a wise man respects them."

—MIRIAM MAKEBA

AFRICA OVERLAND SAFARI

The most fantastic journey of a lifetime. Join private party London/Nairobi via Sahara leaving March. 4 months $1,050 inc. food etc. Tel. London 221-5427 or write M. Calnan, 309 Westbourne Park Rd., London W. 11, U.K.

[Advertisement for the author's trip to Africa—New York Times, 1978.]

Three years at a suburban high school had given me a solid foundational education. But real learning kicked in when my mother offered me another way to learn. "Hey, Peter, want to travel across Africa instead of finishing your senior year of high school?" my mother called out to me from behind the Sunday *New York Times*.

"Umm . . . yes, definitely!"

My mother had seen an ad in the *Times*, and being the adventure-loving spirit she was, and knowing I'd be happy to chuck the remaining months of pointless classes (I had already done well enough to likely be accepted into college), offered me this opportunity.

Africa. The very word sits like a mountain on the page—undefinable, immense, and timeless. To travel through ten countries in 1978 was to witness only a glimpse of this great massive continent and its peoples, but the immersion was deep, the memories burned forever into my heart and soul. I was young, a freshly minted adult; I knew more about self-sufficiency than many my age due to my upbringing, but I knew nothing at all about psychological, emotional, and spiritual self-care for the very same reason. This trip would test me, it would push and pull me, it would offer awe-inspiring natural beauty and painful reality checks. I would make it through but not without major setbacks and what seemed like forces willing me to fail and others saving my life. I embarked on a Heroic Journey all its own in this epic trip—one that I would later look back on as instrumental in defining who I was and who I *wanted* to be.

There were seventeen of us, aged eighteen to forty. I was the youngest, at eighteen, and the only American. Most were English, but some had come from Canada and Australia, and while our differences were many, we all had something in common: a desire for adventure, a need to escape our "regular" lives, a spirit of wonder and curiosity necessary for such a wild ride. We drove in a late 1962 Bedford RL 4x4 truck with a canvas canopy from London through Europe, across the Mediterranean on a ferry from Sicily to Tunis, across the northern tip of Tunisia, through Algeria and the Sahara, to the west coast of Niger, across Nigeria and Cameroon, directly through the jungles of Central African Republic, the Republic of Congo (what was then called Zaire), and Rwanda, all the way to the east side of the continent to Tanzania and Kenya. We camped in tents and cooked our food the entire trip. What was intended to be four months stretched into six months. We were a group of seventeen Brits, Australians, Germans, Irish, and Canadians, but we lost and gained people along the way for various reasons, including the group leader, Michael, who ditched us a third of the way through the trip and whom I never saw again.

[Overland truck the author and crew drove across Africa in 1978.]

As the youngest and only American, I was dubbed "Riff Raff" by Tina and Michael, one of the English couples on the trip. The moniker was part affectionate and part hierarchical in their vestigial imperialism. It was tight living, as I shared a nylon tent with Freck and Bill, the two Australians. Day in and day out we would jostle and sway with every bump and turn for hours in the back of the truck, facing each other, eyes glazed like troops heading into battle. Days of blistering heat were followed by days of torrential rain. The roads were often treacherous and impassable, too slippery from mud to walk on, let alone drive. At that time there were no paved roads across the Sahara Desert, so we followed a string of periodic oil drums and used a map and compass to navigate. We circled the prayer monument in Algeria three times for good luck and safe travels and then wrestled the road south across the wide-open sand and rubble of the Sahara Desert.

The Sahara, once the actual seafloor, is truly an ocean of sand, and it stretched in all directions as far as I could see. At night, the stars and satellites coursed across the heavens like fireflies, so bright we could read books or maps without flashlights. Too beastly hot in the day, we often drove at night under stars and moonlight, keeping to the oil drum track dotting the landscape. Like the corrugation found on the ocean floor, often the desert would have ripples and ruts carved by the wind. The only way to drive this corrugation was to drive fast to stay on top of the ridges or risk shaking the bolts loose on the bumpers. We chose fast, but with serious consequences. Once, unable to stop in time, we hit a deep gully, and every one of us in back was thrown forward suddenly upon impact. Seventeen people, all the gear, and the food hatches under our seats were all thrown into a pile. Despite bruises and an angry tangle of sweaty arms and legs, we were mostly unhurt, aside from Tina's broken toe. She had been smoking a cigarette at the time and upon impact fell against me. Her lit cigarette burned a clean hole in my back as if she were stubbing it out in an ashtray. I felt it for days. In the dusty desert, it stayed relatively dry, but once we hit the tropical jungles of Cameroon days later, the wound began to fester and became a suppurating tropical ulcer—a problem we would deal with in the days to come.

Although seemingly uninhabited, the desert teemed with life. Distant flares from the burning oil and gas towers lit the sky at night like birthday candles on a sandy cake, and tightly strung electrical wires hummed like a plucked guitar string from the vibrating tension of the single-track power lines. Rest stops for lunch and tea would bring visits from indigo-clothed Tuareg tribespeople who would approach tentatively to trade for items we had. The Tuareg herders would appear with goats or camels out of nowhere. Astute desert survivalists, they dug and tended deep wells in the desert, covered with stone, beehive-shaped huts—something to also avoid hitting in the night while driving. Without knowing what they were at first, I ran into one for fun and nearly fell down the dark pit in the dark. I could feel the devil's pull in the chill of the black hole even before I saw it. Someone shouted, and I panicked, grabbing the wall by the door to keep from slipping in with the sand pouring over the edge and into the abyss below.

[Tuareg woman and her child in the middle of the Sahara.]

The desert heat, the dryness, the lack of food, and the constant pummeling from the daily truck travel had us all daydreaming of the west coast beaches of Cameroon, which lay ahead. We fantasized about the couple of weeks of vacation and promised rest on the black volcanic sands of Batoke Beach that awaited us. We talked of building grass huts and living on fresh seafood, basking in hammocks under breezy palm trees.

[Family tent on the edge of the Sahara Desert in Niger.]

However, once we finally reached Niger, and Nigeria, and then Cameroon, we crossed the line and were swallowed by sub-Saharan Africa and the rainy season. We pitched our tents in a flat, wide, dried riverbed and headed to town to restock beer and food supplies. Then, in the distant desert mountains, a sudden rainstorm sent a torrent of water across the hard-packed sand, becoming a churning river. Coming back from eating in town, we saw something white rolling in the dark.

Freck yelled first. "It's a flash flood, get the truck and gear out of there!"

In a mad panic, we pulled up tent stakes and grabbed backpacks and threw them to high ground, and Mike lurched the truck out of the frothing torrent before everything was washed away. We spent the night and the next day looking for lost items along the riverbank and drying out all of our belongings before packing up and heading to Cameroon.

Chapter Seven

If a tree does not know how to dance, the wind will teach it.

—AFRICAN PROVERB

By the time we finally rolled down the dirt roads of Batoke Beach, our long-awaited beach paradise, outside of Victoria, Cameroon, we were in the heart of monsoon season. It rained nonstop for days. Black volcanic sand, while romantic, is as fine as ground pepper and sticks to everything: clothes, shoes, hands, skin, hair—everything. Africa can be stifling hot, but when it rains, it's cold, and we huddled wet and chilled in the cook tent. Historically, this beautiful coastline has held a dark past. Portuguese slave ships anchored off this coast between here and the islands of Principe and Sao Tome, and a heavy pall can be sensed when looking at the strong currents of the sea. The island of Bioko can be seen as a sinister dark spot on the western horizon.

We camped, naively, among the tall coconut palms and between the tin-roofed huts that served as vacation homes for people in the nearest town of Victoria or cities of Douala and the capital, Yaoundé.

[Man carrying firewood in Niger.]

We would hear coconuts as they dropped from fifty feet above us, slipping through the palm fronds with a *swish-swish* before slamming into the tin roofs of the beach huts. *Boom!* Like incoming mortar fire, we stressfully anticipated them dropping all the time. This was a perfect time and place for me to come down with malaria.

Ailing, I tried to walk to the cook tent by the beach. My legs gave out, and I collapsed on the sand. Somebody helped me back into my tent. I ached everywhere: back, neck, legs, arms. Every muscle cramped into a knot. I felt like I had been hit by a truck. My eyes hurt; even blinking took more effort than I had. I kept them closed. The splitting headache made me retch. The rain continued heavily. I heard the rising water from the swamp lapping against my solo tent. I struggled to move my foam pad and my sleeping bag from the puddle in the lower corner and had to lay back down to rest from the effort. I was hungry but couldn't eat. I was thirsty but couldn't drink. A coconut fell and boomed against a roof nearby. I heard moaning and realized that it was coming from me, more alone in the world than I had ever felt in my life.

I had long been preoccupied with the question of how much time I had left on the planet. My dad was benched with his aneurysm when he was twenty-seven years old, and I lived my life waiting for the inevitable. My days spent in that tent did not help; it was always on my mind. When would the sand run out of my hourglass?

Tina, one of the four women in the group, happened to be a nurse, and she came to check on me. I was pale and covered in sweat and shook violently with chills. I told her my back hurt, and she lifted my T-shirt. She was silent and then said, "I will be right back, Raff." She came back some time later with Eric and Jan.

"Raff, can I just look at your back again?" she said, concern in her voice.

I mumbled something as she lifted my shirt and showed them my back. They talked in hushed tones, but they'd seen something they didn't like.

The burn from Tina's cigarette in the desert was now a red suppurating ulcer, with dead white and purple skin around the dark core of my perpetually damp skin. The burn hole was infected, and a red line was tracking around my back to the front of my chest. The poison was spreading and was making me sick along with the malaria. They left to discuss what needed to happen.

The chloroquine pills may have helped minimize the effects of the malaria, but they did not prevent me from getting it. I shivered uncontrollably in my wet sleeping bag and started to hallucinate. Having malaria in a beach jungle with a flooding swamp and incessant rain played tricks with time. Days and nights ran together. Tina was back with Bernie, the coleader, to show him, and then they both left. I just wanted to be left alone to sleep, but I couldn't get warm, even this close to the equator. I curled up in a ball and moaned softly into the wad of clothes I used as a pillow. Tina was back with Jan, and she had a bright torch, a set of scalpels, and antibiotic ointment. Tina explained softly but firmly: "Raff, I need to carve every bit of the infection out, and I may have to go deep. It is going to hurt, but it has to be done." Her tone was serious.

That didn't sound good, but there were not a lot of options. Jan held my hand, and Eric held me down while Tina carved out the edges of the oozing ulcer. I was face down. I felt her start to prick the edges of the wound, and then it seemed she was boring a hole all the way through me. I tried not to cry and buried my face into a twisted towel. Eric and Jan were trying to console me. Tina was digging everything out that was putrid and infected. I think I blacked out.

Malaria and the infection and the swampy, humid air took my mind. I drifted away into another time and place. I was back in Switzerland three weeks earlier, when we were at the long table behind the restaurant with wine and bread and cheese. Everyone was laughing at stories Mike and Bernie were telling. The painted wooden chairs were mismatched and tippy on the flagstone patio. Cows were in the field close to us. I was laughing and loving being with this crazy group of people at a garden restaurant in Switzerland with perfect weather. The valley was steep and dropped away so I couldn't see the village, but I knew it was there. Tina dug the hole deeper. I told her that I thought that was enough, that I was sure she had gotten it all. But back in Switzerland again, I reached for more bread and cheese because I had had too much wine.

"Ok, Raff, we are almost done," she said, somewhat relieved.

It felt like she had gone inches deep into my back. She packed the wider opening in my back with antibiotics and bandaged my back with gauze and tape. The tape didn't stick very well to my sweaty skin, so she wrapped it in a circle around my chest and back to hold the gauze in place. I was still dizzy, and my head throbbed. She told me to lie face down for the rest of the day.

"Do you think you can sleep? Do you want something to eat?" she asked, fully in nurse mode.

I heard voices but I was still time-traveling in Switzerland, and I came back to people hovered over me in the sodden tent.

"I will bring you some soup and bread," Jan said, but I faded out again.

The next day, Eric had spoken to Tobias, the African caretaker of these cabins who had let us camp here, and told him of my malaria. Tobias spoke to the tribal doctor in town and gave Eric a brown bottle for me to drink.

"What's in it?" I asked

"You don't want to know. He said it will fix your malaria fast. He swears by it."

I swallowed three big gulps of the dark, sludgy liquid. It turned out to be hemoglobin serum made from pig blood in the village. Whether it was a placebo effect or not, it made me better the next morning, and two days later, I felt like I was cured (although I came down with malaria back in the States a year later to the day). My back was sore for a while, but the antibiotics had caught the infection in time and the red line stopped tracking. I was miserable but on the mend. To add to the discomfort of malaria, a gouged-out tropical ulcer, and a flooded tent, my flashlight picked up the shadow of a giant spider on the inside of my mosquito net the size of a dinner plate, which turned out to be a large hermit crab that had gotten in and was climbing up the inside of the netting. I tossed him out into the rain, and I was left to soak in my foam sponge mattress alone. I was there without family, but good, kind people had helped me survive the tropical ulcer and the malaria. I was making new friends in the world. While it took weeks to get my strength back fully, I was learning to adjust to life on the road and ready to see more of Africa.

[Coming upon basking hippos on the way to a swimming hole.]

Africa had much more to share with us, and we soon departed the gray-clouded beaches of Batoke and headed east to Central Africa and the mud-rutted roads deeper and deeper into the jungles of Central Africa and Zaire.

Chapter Eight

"The continent is too large to describe. It is a veritable ocean, a separate planet, a varied, immensely rich cosmos. Only with the greatest simplification, for the sake of convenience, can we say 'Africa.' In reality, except as a geographical appellation, Africa does not exist."

—RYSZARD KAPUŚCIŃSKI

The villages in northern Zaire looked like ghost towns. As we drove, we were struck by a strange realization that there were no men between the ages of sixteen and sixty in the villages, just small children and old people. We later found out that in the southern Shaba Province of Zaire, three thousand rebels had just taken hostage and massacred hundreds of Europeans. French and Belgian airborne forces were called in to fight, and all young men were conscripted and sent to the south to fight what was known as the Battle of Kolwezi. When asked, the British Embassy in Yaoundé gave us a 30 percent chance of coming out of Zaire alive.

And then there was the issue of visas. The Zaire Embassy in New York gave me a visa to cross the country and stamped "1 month" into my passport in ink. The Zaire Embassy in London, however, stamped "8 days" in the British and Australian and Canadian passports,

[Jostling a papaya tree to catch the ripe one.]

knowing people could never cross Zaire in eight days and would have to pay fees to renew. We discovered this discrepancy when we were already on the ferry from Dover to Calais. So, inventive and rebellious as we were, we needed to make a significant correction and put a number "2" in front of the "8 days" in the British passports, essentially forging them.

At night, under a flapping windblown nylon tent off the dunes in Calais, a couple of the group leaders used ballpoint pens and lamp black and tried to match the style of each person's passport. Some looked passable, others looked smudged and altered. We knew we would have to get the border guards talking and laughing while they stamped all the passports in a pile, hoping that the bad ones would be overlooked. That time would come in the months ahead.

As friendly as we found the people to be in Cameroon, we found our first day in Central African Republic to be less welcoming. While setting up camp outside the edge of town, we were surprised by a rock thrown from the trees behind us. And then another rock. And another. A gang of ten boys made themselves known and showed their bravery to each other by hurling stones and laughing. This had never happened to us before, and we could feel the tension build. Bill, the tallest of us and an Australian, was livid. He was about to start throwing rocks back—not a good idea, as we were clearly outnumbered. If we fought back, others would come, and this could all end very badly. I struck on a crazy idea. I said, "Let me try something first."

I went out to the center of the clearing between them and our tents, and I started jumping up and down like a pogo stick, shouting "Boing, boing, boing!" The children looked at each other and then back at me bouncing up and down. They dropped their rocks and came closer. The largest boy broke into a smile, and then he started pogo-sticking and yelling "Boing, boing, boing!" also. Freck and Bill saw how this changed the energy, and they started jumping up and down too. Soon, we had all the kids and all of us pogo-sticking and laughing and "boing, boinging" in the clearing in the middle of Central Africa. Crisis averted, and peace was achieved for the time being.

The wet clay roads across Central Africa and Zaire were rutted so deeply that entire cargo trucks would disappear into them, lumber through, and, if lucky, come out the other side. Other holes or bridge crossings were impassable, and hundreds of trucks would line up on both sides of the hole waiting to get through for days. Once in Zaire, we determined that loading the truck on a barge and traveling up the

[Looking for a lost key in the mud where the truck broke down and drinking a lot of beer.]

Congo River from Bumba to Kisangani was the only way we could get through.

It was an exciting time and a different way to travel. One large ferry would strap six or eight barges to the sides of its flanks and then navigate the whole raft upriver. At night, when we traveled, a large lighthouse beacon on the ferry roof swung like a living flashlight, searching for painted markers on the riverbanks and looking for indications of sandbars that formed periodically. A few of us found a way to get up on the roof, and we would sit near the beacon and watch the navigation from a hundred feet up. The Indian captain liked us as a group but warned that it was not safe. If he ever hit a sandbar, the boat would stop suddenly, and we would be thrown to our deaths since there were no railings. We appreciated his concern but ignored his suggestion. Free from mosquitoes and enjoying the breeze and the night stars, our nights on the rooftop gave us a unique view of the jungle, with giant robotic searchlights beaming ahead into the primordial forest, tranquil and terrifying in its all-encompassing darkness.

One night, I came down from the roof to take pictures of the barges in the setting sun, and I set up my tripod with the camera for a time-lapse photograph. It was then that we hit the sandbar. Total chaos ensued. Barges split away from the ferry and drifted downriver. People fell overboard in the dark, shouting for help. A rusted cable snapped and whipped my camera tripod over and would have killed me had I still been standing right there. The ferry captain jammed the barges onto the sandbar more firmly and then disconnected us to go down the fast river to get the other barges. We watched as people were rescued and brought back on the boat, and we could see the light beam on the ferry sweeping downriver for the other barges and for people knocked into the water from the impact of the sandbar.

The captain was right. Had we been on the roof, we would have all been killed. Had I still been standing by the camera, I would have been killed. Once all the boats and barges were reconnected, we continued our journey upriver.

Impenetrable walls of green jungle bordered the Congo River, with occasional smoke from hidden villages. Life seemed simpler, less complicated, than my life in New York. The thought occurred to me: What if I dove in? What if I swam to shore? Providing nothing ate me on my swim to the riverbank, might I live happier in a quiet village?

I was intoxicated by Africa. The sky alone was worth the price of admission. We traveled up the Congo River without incident and disembarked at Kisangani. As we climbed into the mountains of Rwanda, I was reminded again of Switzerland. The cool mist in the mornings hung like a minty fog in the eucalyptus trees along the red clay roads. The high-cheekboned faces of the villagers smiled and waved and laughed at us for going down the wrong road, laughing again as they got to wave to us a second time.

[Woman in Rwanda carrying firewood.]

We bumped and lurched along the rutted roads from Rwanda into the low plains of Tanzania, with the lure of the game parks ahead. We were out of food, living on cooked cabbage, chicken broth cubes, and tea. I had already lost ten of the fifteen pounds I would lose by the end of the trip. The truck broke down again, and we waited in the dusty car park in Mwanza, camping in our tents. Every night for two weeks, we each took two-hour shifts of guard duty to protect our vulnerable little tent village in the middle of the city. The truck finally repaired, and us cranky and dusty from living in the dustbins of the city, we drove past the outskirts of Mwanza and on to the game parks in eastern Tanzania.

[Freck, Peter, Mike, and Bill outside the dusty tents where the author and crew camped in Mwanza.]

Restless from waiting weeks for truck parts, we drove all day to the Serengeti, arriving at night with the game reserve officially closed. Tired and grubby, we pitched our tents on the plains within the Serengeti, knowing full well we were in animal country. Despite the night sounds of baboon troops, elephants and other herd animals, and prowling lions, we were left undisturbed and woke to a blood-orange Serengeti sunrise, eager for the day.

Someone, probably one of the Australians, coined the acronym MAMOFA: miles and miles of fucking Africa. After the long trek on slippery roads, weeks of rain, malaria, traveling through cholera outbreaks, and smearing ourselves with diesel to keep the mosquitoes at bay in the jungle, the savanna was fresh and open and welcome.

I would sit high on the truck roof, my long Mowgli hair held back in a headband, and silently commune with the land and animals. My

[Hyaena at dusk on the Serengeti National Park.]

young, eager eyes could often spot the animals hiding before the others in the group, and I would call out:

"Wildebeest."

"Zebra and giraffe."

"Cape buffalo under the trees at three o'clock."

Thomson's gazelles, with their racing stripes, and Grant's gazelles, seemingly more sophisticated, all faced different directions to make their individual shapes indistinguishable to predators. Baboon troops huddled under the acacia trees in twos, threes, and twenties. Warthogs, with their thin tail flags up, trotted like they had mail to deliver. Secretary birds and storks strutted like they were discussing a verdict. In the distance, the hulking masses of the Cape buffalo and the elephants ripped branches down from trees. Hyenas, with their spotted coats and back legs shorter for long loping runs, looked like they were spoiling for a fight.

This was Eden, I thought. This was heaven. This was how the world looked before humans arrived and messed things up: rhinos in Ngorongoro Crater, more elephants in Lake Manyara, and the birds—all the pink flamingoes taking off at once in a blurry, pink, raucous flurry.

I became a part of Africa, and Africa became a deep part of me on this trip. It seeped into my soul: the light, the immense land, the glorious skies. After crossing it in my teenage years, I took with me something of everything I saw and felt. The loneliness and the majesty. The beauty of the sunsets and daily humanity of human joy and suffering. Crossing Africa, like crossing the Atlantic Ocean, or climbing a high mountain, is something that can be survived but never conquered. Getting malaria, suffering a tropical ulcer, nearly falling into a deep well in the Sahara—I didn't know it at the time, but these adventures were gifts. Experiences I can look back on as elements that shaped my later years. I left that continent with greater fortitude, with a sense of myself.

Crossing Africa was the Heroic Journey that helped me get through even harder times to come. It was my fallback: "I can do this . . . I crossed Africa."

Chapter Nine

"When you leave Africa, as the plane lifts, you feel that more than leaving a continent you're leaving a state of mind. Whatever awaits you at the other end of your journey will be of a different order of existence."

—FRANCESCA MARCIANO

Three weeks home from Africa, my head still spinning and my heart still raw, I was whisked up to the green grass quads of a small private college, with squeaky-clean, predominantly white kids from the East Coast of the United States. I didn't yet know about Joseph Campbell's work—how to frame my time in Africa as useful, or reenter "normal life" with newfound purpose and perspective. My journey in Africa ended abruptly, like a needle scratched across a record, and I flailed in the aftermath.

Some journeys take a lifetime to unpack.

St. Lawrence University in upstate New York offered me a partial scholarship and, it being close to home and with no other offers, I accepted. I triple majored in government, anthropology, and creative writing and double majored in drinking and relationships. Life at college should have been about learning what was important, what wasn't, and how to manage my time. Instead, it was a four-year odyssey of drinking, drugging, and relationships as I struggled to discover who I was.

One particularly bright spot was my freshman year writing class with author and Fiction International founder Joe David Bellamy. Through Joe David Bellamy, I met famous authors like T. Coraghessan Boyle and Paul Fussell. Lorrie Moore was his former student, and these amazing writers loomed large as people I wanted to follow. I read Jayne Anne Phillips, E. L. Doctorow, Thomas McGuane, John McPhee, and Breece D'J Pancake. I was smitten with the craft of writing and the world of writers. After I read my first short story aloud, there was silence in the class. "If you can write three hundred words like that, you will never have to work a day in your life," Joe said. I then spent the next dozen years trying to live up to that compliment and write as well as that again.

If only my engagement in classes had been enough for me to feel purposeful. Still in pursuit of positive attention, I swung the tiller hard over into the realm of overachiever. I ran the International House, a campus theme house of students who had traveled with school programs; was the head of the Mohawk Akwesasne Tutoring program; hosted an international peer-review paper competition; held a part-time job at the snack bar; and tried to maintain multiple relationships and a social affiliation at the ATO fraternity. I pulled all-nighters to get exams and term papers done, and I drank and drugged through it all. I thought if I took on just a little bit more responsibility, I might be seen as a worthwhile human being. If I could juggle three things, why not four, or seven, or twelve.

Things began to spin out of control. I began having blackouts. I woke up in the middle of conversations with professors without a clue about what we were discussing. I woke up while driving someone else's yellow Pontiac convertible in the pouring rain, with a car full of people—and the signs were all in French. I had driven in a blackout to Montreal. I woke up another time at dusk—or was it dawn—asking people what day it was. And then my paranoia kicked in, and I started to avoid and fear people. Drinking changed my perspective; it made me withdraw when I couldn't control how much I drank. I stopped talking to people. I hid in my room, or in the library. I missed important deadlines. I screwed up important events. I forgot things I was supposed to do. I let people down. I was once again the kid on a fence over a freeway, and I was losing my grip.

Trying to succeed in the daytime and then undermining my own effectiveness by drinking at night became an ever-tightening spiral. I couldn't breathe. On the recommendation of a therapist during my junior year, I took my January interterm out at our family summer house on Block Island, Rhode Island, to recuperate.

Block Island is a small jewel in the Atlantic, a pork chop–shaped island only twenty-one square miles, surrounded by rocky beaches on the north, west, and south, and a two-mile stretch of perfect white sand on the east. Over the years, I've spent thirty summers there. In January, it is mostly boarded up except for about two hundred year-round residents, the library, and one supermarket. I walked beaches, wrote short stories and poetry, and read a lot of Hemingway. In the drafty, unheated house in the middle of the island, I developed a relationship with a French coal stove. She needed constant tending. She clicked and groaned as I learned the secrets of keeping her glowing. I slept in the living room, with sheets of plastic hanging up to close off the doorways to the rest of the house. I hauled a driftwood log up from the beach and started to carve it in the living room, woodchips flying from the chisel. I found solace in the isolation of the island that winter: the constant wave action of the ocean against the land; the weather and birds blown in by storm clouds; the crashing of waves up on the beach, the hissing of the waves receding, pulling back all they brought almost as a second thought; the gulls dipping low over the water, just skimming the surface; and the plaintive cry of the lone gull on the bleached town dock.

I could hear my own inner voice calling out to the world to be seen or found or loved. The island felt welcoming; it seemed to know I was hurting, that I needed a break. My world started to slow down. I worked for a carpenter named Joe and helped him tend his sheep, shovel coal into forty-pound bags, and repair stone walls. I remember the sweet steamy breath of the sheep in the barn, the murmuring of a flock of sheep all standing around waiting for oats, my boots wobbly on frozen ground, bringing them buckets of water from the cistern, the starry night above and hard ruts on the ground below. I felt two hundred years old, connected to every person who had ever tended animals in the winter.

The gray winter Atlantic coast brought me back to reality. I chopped wood. I carried water. I listened to Vivaldi violin concertos. I limited my drinking to only beer and wine. I slowly regained my sense of self. I crawled back from the cliff edge of an emotional breakdown. I went back to college in hopes of keeping my life more balanced.

I was better for a little while, but the self-confidence of living alone on the island did not last. As graduation approached, I had no idea what I would do next. The night of graduation, I slept on the bare mattress ticking on my bed in my college dorm, covered by a big gray coat I had bought at the Salvation Army store, what we called "Salvation Armani"—a fitting send-off for my new life. Four years at school had been a wonderful growing experience, and yet the working world called, and I was at a loss. I still fancied myself a writer ever since that freshman class, but I didn't think I was good enough to make a living at it. I remember walking the halls of the Religious Studies Department with no idea what I would do after graduation. I saw a bulletin about a language program at Cornell, and it seemed a worthy port to pull into to avoid the tumultuous storm of indecision.

I applied to Cornell Graduate School and was accepted in their Foreign Asian Language Concentration program in Indonesian language. I just missed receiving the tuition grant and so deferred for a year so I could be up at Cornell with the full Title VI language study grant. I returned to Block Island to find a job and wait a year for graduate school.

I had kept it together long enough to graduate, but once back on Block Island, with no job and no real prospects, I quickly unraveled. I secured jobs with master carpenter-builders John and Joe, both with deep roots on the island. The work was hard, and fun, and I gained a second liberal arts education from those two guys, learning everything from pouring cement for foundations and framing to sidewall shingling and roofing.

It was the first time I had spent the entire year on Block Island and experienced the summer wind down, when the families packed up and left for school. The winds picked up, beaches emptied, houses boarded up, and stores closed for the season. The hardy few who stayed ran into each other at the post office. I worked with Joe all that summer, fall, and winter—long hours, mostly outdoors, in any weather.

Every night, I would get home and try to write a story or a poem, drink a few beers, and then read. Hemingway came to mind again and again—for his struggle with depression, for his deft hand at simple, clean writing. I was also reminded of two quotes of his that I typed out and pinned over my desk:

"Alcohol dulled the blades of my perception."
"Now he would never write the things that he had saved to write until he knew enough to write them well."[2]

---

2 Ernest Hemingway, *The Snows of Kilimanjaro, and Other Stories*. (Charles Scribner's, 1970).

These phrases haunted me as I drank each evening with my typewriter. In many of Hemingway's stories, men came to terms with the choices they made in their lives and, upon reflection, what they wished they had done differently.

My last drink wasn't due to an all-night blackout or a weeklong bender. My last drink was the sad, tired realization that I couldn't keep doing this. That I would never amount to much and achieve any of my hopes and dreams. I still fancied myself a writer . . . but I was still lost and grasping at straws. Alcohol made me live drink to drink, and even the sober times were depressing. A friend once said, "You aren't a writer, you just drink with your typewriter."

My last drink was a half beer, and the rest I poured down the sink. I just couldn't do it anymore. I was beat. I lost the ability to keep fighting it. Finally, on August 21, 1982, I surrendered to the fact that maybe, just maybe, I couldn't go on drinking. And I didn't know how to stop. My mother had entered a Twelve-Step program a couple of years earlier and said there were meetings on the island. Her brother John had joined AA ten years before, and they both attended meetings regularly. That night I went to my first Saturday Night Meeting on Block Island and began to climb out of the hole that I had dug in my life.

I drove down Water Street and past the National Hotel and Bar and up the familiar hill of the Harbor Baptist Church. The church overlooks Ballard's, and I could hear people yelling over the music. It was dusk. I didn't really want to be driving to a meeting, but I had a strange feeling that it was the right thing to do. I kept going. I parked my rusty green Bronco on the grass and walked up to the back door. There was a metal sign on the door: a circle with a blue triangle, code for an AA meeting without saying AA meeting. Inside it was warm and steamy with coffee and teapots. People pulled chairs around tables and hugged and exchanged greetings with each other. I felt like I'd stumbled into a private dinner party. An older guy came up to me and reached out to shake my hand.

"Are you new?" he asked.

"Yes."

"Welcome. You're in the right place," he said.

He called over his shoulder and told everyone my name was Peter and I was new. More friendly people greeted me. I still wanted to leave, but they gave me a cup of instant coffee and showed me into the library, with plush pink and yellow chairs and a long couch. I put on my best face and tried to be friendly, but I was a bit dazzled by it all. In my greetings, I mentioned that I was Kay's son, and they nodded with recognition. They all knew her. The meeting started with a couple of readings. I was in my body and then out of my body, watching myself sit there in a brightly lit church library with a circle of people who all seemed to be happy and earnest. I tried to be happy and earnest too. It was fascinating.

I read a section of a blue book that was passed around. As I listened to people speak, they expressed feelings that I had felt. They were describing things that I had done. People were laughing at the foolishness of their previous thoughts and behaviors. Then they were quiet as they held space for the pain someone had been through. There was joy, there was gratitude. There was honest, vulnerable sharing. Then it was my turn. I told them what I had been going through, and they listened with interest. They nodded at similar feelings they had had, and they told me it would get better and to keep coming back. Another person spoke and then we all stood in a circle holding hands saying a closing prayer. I felt shy, but at the same time, I felt at home. Like I was home. Like I belonged there with these newly met people: artists, sailors, carpenters, shop owners, and chefs. We returned to the kitchen and washed cups in the sink, restacked the books, and trickled out into the night. I had done it, my first AA meeting. It felt good—no, it felt amazing. I was electric with possibility. For the first time, I thought I could do this. All I had to do was not drink one day at a time and then come back. I had a pocket full of people's names scribbled on bits of paper with their numbers, new friends on a new journey, and I was not crazy and I was not alone.

While I had had a relatively short drinking and drugging run, from thirteen to twenty-two, I had gone at it hard and with a vengeance. Yes, I had a drinking problem, but I told myself I did it with class. I don't know many college kids who maintained a wine rack, kept Cointreau and Remy Martin on the bookshelf, and had Stolichnaya vodka in the freezer in their dorm room. Drinking was such a part of my life that the parameters of propriety blurred. I would bring a bottle of Grand Marnier to the library and pour out a snifter as I wrote my term papers on the upper deck of a study carrell. Wasn't I living the life? Wasn't this what everyone did? "Always star in your own movie" was a quote I learned, and I lived it to the max. Every sunset was accompanied by a bottle of red wine. Sunday mornings meant Bloody Marys. I choreographed my life around getting ready to drink, drinking in the most cinematic way, and then recovering from drinking.

In addition to the Montreal blackout, I had a run-in with the police at the 1980 Lake Placid Olympics. After driving past roadblocks and trying to get close to the action, I found myself blackout drunk with a cop holding me up against the side of my Bronco, threatening me to get out of town or he would lock me up. At a college fraternity hazing, I was forced to drink seventeen shots of cheap bourbon whiskey, and I was blind drunk. I jumped out of a moving car and ran down the road to get away from the older fraternity brothers. A big guy named Dirk caught up to me and tackled me on the dirt road, grinding my face into the gravel. The whole left side of my face was scraped raw and seeped blood and plasma for days. I must have raised eyebrows as I sat in class dabbing at the road marks on my face, but I don't remember. We did lose friends in college to drugging and drinking. One of the sweetest guys was sitting on the edge of a dam, high as a kite, and laughed as he fell into the water. To the horror of those with him, he was sucked by the sluice into the dam and never seen again.

That night at the AA meeting, I started my life all over again—at twenty-two years old. I attended four meetings a week that first year: Mondays, Wednesdays, Fridays, and Saturdays. I had lots to learn and, more importantly, lots to unlearn. Stopping drinking in the middle of my first summer out of college was a strange thing, but drinking and drugging had run its course. I was utterly exhausted. I surrendered.

As romantic as I perceived drinking to be, I had to reimagine my life without it. No more sunsets with a bottle of wine and a budding relationship. No more "hair of the dog" drinking to ease a hangover. I needed to start all over again—new game, new rule book, new life. I found myself getting stronger each day, not in willpower, but in my ability to surrender. As soon as I admitted I didn't know how to live this way, wisdom came at me from the sober community. I came into the meetings to stop drinking, but I stayed to learn how to live. Winter days were spent working on houses, tending Joe's sheep and cattle, and then keeping a house warm with a small coal stove. As spring came, I saw the blooming of shad trees and the warming candle smell of bayberry bushes as signs that I was going to make it. The salt air was in my blood, and I began to appreciate the dawning of my new life. I worked one more summer and then prepared for graduate school and a program in Indonesian language at Cornell University. I had been around the world; now was a time to go deeper and learn an Asian language that would add to my eclectic life tool kit.

Chapter Ten

"He who fights with monsters might take care lest he thereby become a monster. And if you gaze for long into an abyss, the abyss gazes also into you."

—**FRIEDRICH NIETZSCHE**

[Dark times in New York City.]

After graduate school, at Cornell, where I studied Indonesian language and audited the MFA program in writing, I headed back to New York City. As a major hub on the Eastern Seaboard, New York looms large like the Emerald Kingdom, and growing up in Westchester, as I did, the city was always the natural draw. When I first moved there, I was amazed at how tired I was. It all seemed so unnatural: the noise, the constant sirens, flashing lights, car alarms, taxis honking, and incessant clammer. The pounding from walking on pavement made my feet and legs hurt. How could people only live in cement and glass buildings, and walk on cement sidewalks, and look up at only a sliver of sky above?

Over time, the city lights, buildings, and billboards faded, like rain-blurred chalk drawings. The sounds became familiar, even comforting, with an air of expectant possibility, like an orchestra tuning up, the city symphony launching into a day. When I paused to really look, the windows revealed dance classes in front of mirrors, families growing tomatoes on fire escapes, children doing homework at kitchen tables, lonely people watching TV in dark rooms, musicians and opera singers practicing scales that echoed in alleyways. The city was alive, and it smoldered with possibility and creativity everywhere.

Life was a mix of cultures everywhere. Koreans ran fruit markets. Indians ran newsstands. Greeks had coffee shops, Italians the pizzerias. West Africans sold fake Louis Vuitton purses and fake Rolexes by Rockefeller Center and Penn Station.

In the late '80s, I ran with a fun group of sober people and New York was romantic: playing pool at Julian's on 14th Street or hitting a meeting on the Upper West Side. By focusing on getting sober, we felt we were immune to the other responsibilities of life. We were working on ourselves, and that somehow gave us carte blanche to stay up all night, explore the art world, audition to be in Off-Off-Broadway shows, study improv at Chicago City Limits, fall in and out of relationships, and search for the next best, cheapest apartments.

My first job in New York was as a lead list telemarketer, selling supposedly verified sales leads to stockbrokers in a boiler-room environment. A bus took me from Penn Station to Hackensack, New Jersey, and we dialed our fingers to the bone. It was ten years before the film *Glengarry Glen Ross* came out, but I lived it. I was selling across the country and got paid cash every week in an envelope. We rang a bell when we made a sale. When I realized that the company was misrepresenting what they were selling, I quit.

I switched to working with a nonprofit leading youth leadership and wilderness programs based on Outward Bound principles in the South Bronx. I commuted from Manhattan to the South Bronx by subway, often consuming a Gray's Papaya drink or a Yoo-hoo and a hot dog.

With my Block Island carpentry skills, I renovated offices and apartments on the Upper East Side. Evenings were spent with sober friends, AA meetings, and restaurants on the Upper West Side, working with others. Working on myself.

A group of us guys from the program called ourselves the GD Club as a way to bolster our resolve and not backslide into recent bad relationships. We would coach each other to resist calling up old girlfriends every time we felt lonely. We scraped up enough money to eat at China Latina or Dallas BBQ and unpack our lives through despair and laughter about the "demons" we were fighting that day. But for some, the demons were deadly. We lost three of the seven guys to suicide. Their demons won. It made the rest of us cling more tightly to the program, chilled by the looming alternatives.

My demons were cunning and patient, toying with me when I least expected it. While renovating a therapist's office on the seventh floor in Chelsea, I noticed a woman sunbathing nude on the rooftop across the alley. The voices in my head said that I could jump from the window to the water tower and then climb up to where she was on the roof.

Suddenly, for some reason, she put her clothes back on and left the roof. That night you did not see a guy on the ten o'clock news who died while jumping to a water tower from the seventh floor.

[St. Marks Place, New York City.]

On weekends, I went rock climbing up at the Shawangunk Mountains in New Paltz, New York. Not surprisingly, given my tree- and bridge-climbing experience, I took to rock climbing like a mountain goat. Every boulder, every crag made me pause as I traced a likely route up their faces. I even looked at every building in the city as a challenge to get at least a few feet off the ground.

Being in nature helped quiet my demons, but they were always there in the back of my mind, riding the thermals like circling vultures. To calm and appease them, I would sometimes ride the subway between the train cars. I suffered tinnitus and ringing in my ears, and the screech of the metal wheels on the metal tracks in a porcelain-tiled subway station would leave me reeling. It was so painfully loud, so piercing, it made me crazy. So crazy, I had to embrace the dragon and go deeper into the noise, flashing lights, and steam.

I pushed through the crowd to get close to the doors but not too close to the tracks. My demons wanted me to jump as the train pulled into the station, but I wouldn't give them that easy satisfaction. *Not today*, I told them. Impatient for the train to stop and the doors to open, I waited. People exited like lemmings, and I pushed in. I cut to the right, headed for the front door. It was heavy like a submarine hatch. I turned the handle and pulled hard. Once outside, I relaxed. I grabbed the safety bars on the back of the car in front and on the front of the car in back as we bumped and jostled. The coupling mechanism took up slack and the cars lurched forward. We were off and gathering speed. The wind was slow and hot at first, then it hit the opposing wind from the #2 express train and roared like a tornado. From somewhere deep inside me, from my primal core, I started to moan and then to scream. I was howling in the tunnel at the jolt and roar of the train, the sparks and flashbulb lights and sudden pockets of pitch black between stations, the shrick of the train as the wheels careened and rubbed metal raw. *Clackety-clackety-clack.* I wailed into the madness, releasing all the things in hell flying out at once from somewhere deep inside me. Something dark and in pain—no, not just pain: anguish. *Clackety-clackety-clack.* Black wind blasted through ghosts of steam, flashes and sparks, and the dead rat smell of hell. The steel plates of the train foyers separated, collided, and ground as I clung to the bucking dragon. In the clamor, I found calm. No one could hear me. The dragon and the demons and I were one. The train braked with a jolt and slowed. The dragon got quiet, just one more long screech as we come into the stop at 42nd Street. I inhaled the wet, burned smell of the city's underbelly, the fetid air of the tunnels. We stopped short, and I fixed my hair before I pushed through the hatch door and exited with the crowd. A couple looked surprised to see me coming from outside the train car. But I was spent and serene. My demons had had their choir practice, and they were, for the moment, at peace.

These were times my family never saw. I didn't want them to know of the times of pain, self-doubt, and depression that befell me. But I was not alone. The city was full of people wrestling with demons. You could see it in their eyes or hear it in their whispers as they shuffled along the street. Those of us attempting to get sober would drag ourselves to church-basement meetings or upstairs over dance halls to hear life stories worse than ours, to sip coffee and nibble cookies, and to get a glimmer of hope that we had beat the demons another day and were still sober, despite everything.

Chapter Eleven

"Both giving and receiving forgiveness are pure expressions of radical compassion. Both evolve us. When we open in forgiveness, we reconnect with our own openheartedness."

—TARA BRACH

While I was a student of relationships, I can't say I was a *good* student. Time after time, I stuck my finger in the proverbial spinning fan, trying to make relationships work. Addicted to women and romance made me fun at the beginning, but the Peter Pan/Huck Finn persona in me found it hard to be in a relationship, and I can imagine girlfriends found it hard to be with me. Throughout college and then my early adult life, I struggled to sustain what I learned later was necessary for honest, authentic relationships. Even before I knew about my romance addiction, it seemed to show up in my early college poetry:

Won't You Come to Dinner?

Won't you come to dinner?
I will feed you my poetry.
You may think it half-baked
But I like it.

Won't you come to dinner?
I will cook for you a dream world.
Exotic as cumin and coriander,
Soft as a vanilla beach.

Not much to eat, you say?
Why I've lived grandly as a king
On such fare as this
All winter long.

My five years of living in New York City were like a Shakespearean play, with me as the hopeless romantic. Like D'Artagnan of *The Three Musketeers* or James Bond, I was chivalrous and infatuated with falling in love. But the romance each time was short-lived. I was easily distracted. I spotted the prettiest woman in the room and sought her heart like a medieval courtier. Yet my own growing self-awareness had begun to stir, and I knew something was amiss.

I longed for stability, projecting into my own future and seeing the loneliness that this type of relational pursuit would provide.

My own self-condemnation was the beginning, but it took years of therapy and recovery before I began to understand the deep tectonic plates shifting in my emotional realm. Based on my childhood, a loving but erratic homelife, and early sexual exploration blowing open portals of intimacy that never hinged quite right again, it was no wonder I was addicted to romance and falling in love. Seeking to bolster my own self-esteem by getting women to think I was wonderful, I yearned for love and gave away my soul. In futile attempts to cover deep insecurities, I would dance my heart out to appear magical and unique.

After five years of living on the edge, I finally made a break from New York and moved half of everything I owned in a 1970 red Ford pickup truck to Minnesota. I got my Master of Science in experiential education and was hired at the Voyageur Outward Bound School to run their urban youth program.

I kept dating, kept seeking that love connection, and eventually I married a woman I met at Outward Bound. She was an outdoor wilderness educator, who lifted my loaded Madden eighty-pound mountaineering pack onto her back with one quick swing and whose only comment was "Ooh . . . heavy."

I thought she was great: tough, smart, and she worked with the deaf in a charter school. I worked hard to win her affection, and yet somehow, I knew on our honeymoon that I had made a mistake. We were so different. I looked at every day as a possibility of a miracle whereas she expected the worst, so she wouldn't be disappointed. If I bumped my head on the kitchen cabinet, she would laugh at me. She focused on the specific details of life, and I was more drawn to the creative art of life. For some, this would have been a perfect combination, but for us, it became an ever-widening chasm of unbridgeable perspectives. How had I missed seeing all that? A year later, we moved into our first home, and things worked for a time with the buzz of the newness of marriage and homelife. A year later, we were blessed with a baby girl, who gave us focus and direction and gave me the chance to be the father I never really had and had always wanted to be. As distance grew between us as parents, we put more focus on our daughter, and she became our world.

In an attempt to improve the relationship, we headed off to Indonesia to run a corporate leadership program for a tin-mining company. In the two years we were there, we drifted further and further apart and, despite having a second wonderful child, our son, in Perth, Western Australia, we realized we were not going to make it as a couple. We were just too different.

After two years living in Indonesia, we moved back to the States and our home in Minnesota. I found an apartment two blocks away so I could be close to the kids. Despite both of our efforts to be civil, most communication with her was strained and triggering. It has taken years to soften.

A few more years went by with shared custody and kid swapping every week. As the kids grew, it became even more evident how different we were as people and as parents. How was I going to impart my important values if I only had the kids half the time? It seemed to take two to three days to unwind their mom's attitudes and behaviors, and then they would go back. The only message I could consistently deliver was that I loved the kids very, very much, and I would never leave them. I was always, always going to be their father. Their mother and I were just not good partners together.

After the divorce and a two-year blur of romantic dating and soulmate searching, I began to learn to live more grounded as a single parent. I studied Interplay Dance, an improvisational and poetic open form of expression that freed me to get more in touch with who I was and gave me a glimpse of some of my inner gifts. Just when I heard myself saying, *See, I am good at not being in a relationship*, a woman from Prince Edward Island appeared on the scene of my dance class. Completely different from my ex-wife, this woman was soft, kind, and generous of spirit.

She came at the perfect time for the kids. We committed to being the best we could be as individuals and as a couple. I had a second chance as a married partner, and I put everything into marriage number two. She was a soft place in a hard world, which I told her often. The kids adored her and blossomed in the growing light of her gentle love.

However, despite our best intentions, differences emerged that were irreconcilable. Her stress manifested into body pain, which nothing could cure, despite crossing the country for the latest tests, remedies, and neuropathy trials. The ongoing undiagnosable pain began to wear us both down. What began as kindness and mutual respect began to fray, and blame for pain was sought. I became the target and the cause, and without understanding the rationale for that, it divided us irreparably.

We divorced after eight years. I was tired and frustrated from six years of caretaking and frustrated and confused that whatever caused the pain had been attributed to me. I left that relationship more resolutely committed to living on my own. The emotional toll from both failed marriages spun me into a dark place, highlighted by the caustic comments from my kids who couldn't understand why this had happened again.

My daughter's tearful accusation of "Dad, what is wrong with you?" burned a hole in my heart. I asked myself the same question. What *was* wrong with me? Why was I unable to pick good partners, or *be* a good partner, and live a fruitful, loving life like people did in the movies? I pursued men's groups, and therapy, and drum circles. I immersed myself in my work. I'd spent thirty years working in the leadership development field, and I was good at that. I worked harder and traveled more. I swore I would never be in a relationship again. I had had enough. My divorces devastated me. They challenged all the norms I had heard as a child about what it means to be a family. Despite seeing my mother's separation from my father, and her failed second marriage, I thought I would be immune. It wouldn't happen to me. Divorcing a second time was easier in some ways and harder in others. I knew I didn't want to live a life of misery. I knew that I had choices. If we truly could not resolve our differences, then at least let us part courteously, if not amicably. The hard part was being a "two-time loser." What *was* wrong with me?

Then came marriage number three. I had been in leadership development for a long time and wanted to add more skills to my program delivery repertoire. I explored new tools, new adventure experiences, and equine therapy as a powerful practice for group dynamics. After a lot of research with local practitioners, I learned there was a wide range of ways to deliver equine facilitation. I contacted an old friend on the East Coast who was in the equine leadership field and asked him for any recommendations for facilitators in Minnesota. He gave me Tanya's name, and I reached out to find out more about what it took to do this type of work. Over the course of a half-dozen meetings in as many months, we agreed that there might be a way our leadership firm could partner with animals in the respectful way that she practiced. Over the months of meetings, it surfaced that she was also in the midst of a divorce. That summer, she helped plant all the flowers in my backyard and by November, we were married. On November 11, 2011. At 11:11 a.m. Seriously. 11-11-11 at 11:11 a.m.

When I speak of Tanya, I often paraphrase Billy Crystal's line on New Year's Eve from the film *When Harry Met Sally*: "When you meet the person you want to spend the rest of your life with . . . you want the rest of your life to start right now."

Once our respective divorces were finalized, we both stepped easily into our new relationship. Tanya was a social worker and had worked with youth for years. She was very clear that she wanted to let her relationship with my kids develop over time. She had no intention of pretending she was a new mother to them. They had a mother, and a second stepmother, with whom they were still close. She built a relationship with each by consistently showing up for them as a loving and caring adult. In time, both kids grew to respect and lovc her.

When my mother came down with cancer in 2016, we were devastated. Even though she lived in Maine and we lived in Minnesota, we were on the phone with her daily, and we would travel there or she would join us for holidays. Along the way, Tanya began to get a strange inkling that she had something as well. She knew that the sore throat she had was not an ordinary thing. Our journey together was already tested by her deep twenty-four seven dedication to her academic pursuit of a doctorate in social work, and it ratcheted up even higher with the discovery that she had cancer, too. Life kept challenging us, as we moved houses from the center of the metro area to the northern outskirts. And then the COVID pandemic hit the scene. While this was shattering, we learned to stay connected through it all. We grounded ourselves in knowing that we could get through anything.

In the crucible of life's challenges, I was beginning to change. Whereas I had been a reluctant caretaker with my second wife's undiagnosed neuropathy pain, I learned how to be a devoted care*giver* of Tanya through her darkest days.

I also learned to take care of myself in the process, to reach out to people for support and ask for help. The differences we shared became more clearly understandable through Insights Discovery™, a psychometric communication tool based on Carl Jung's research. I was ill-equipped in my prior marriages to appreciate the gifts of our differences and only watched frustrated from the sidelines as they became insurmountable, and the marriages unraveled.

I had continued in AA all these years, and through the Twelve-Step program, I found acceptance for the life I had led—that every twist and turn that led me to this place happened for a reason. A former colleague of mine once said of her own cancer journey: "Life happens *for* us, not to us." I had come to that realization too. I was living the dream I had always wanted. I was becoming the man I had always wanted to be.

My life now continues to benefit from the practice of reframing. My third marriage is still going strong, after thirteen years. I am over forty-two years sober, due to the grace of my Higher Power that I choose to call God, the generous selfless gifts of my fellow program members, and my own feeble but dedicated practice of the Twelve Steps. I live with Tanya, a loving partner—different from me in many ways, thank God.

The attention-seeking boy in me who crossed bridges and had to be the class clown has learned to value himself from the inside out. The lonely, heartsick lover has learned to nurture his own spirit without seeking affirmations from other people. The distraction caused by addictions and the pursuit of temporary pleasures has been replaced by a deeper understanding of what I want in life and who I am as a noble person.

All of the most painful parts of my life I have had to reframe, to recategorize for the rites of passage they provided me and the learnings that stay with me to this day.

PART THREE:

THE HEROIC JOURNEY, EXPLAINED AND APPLIED

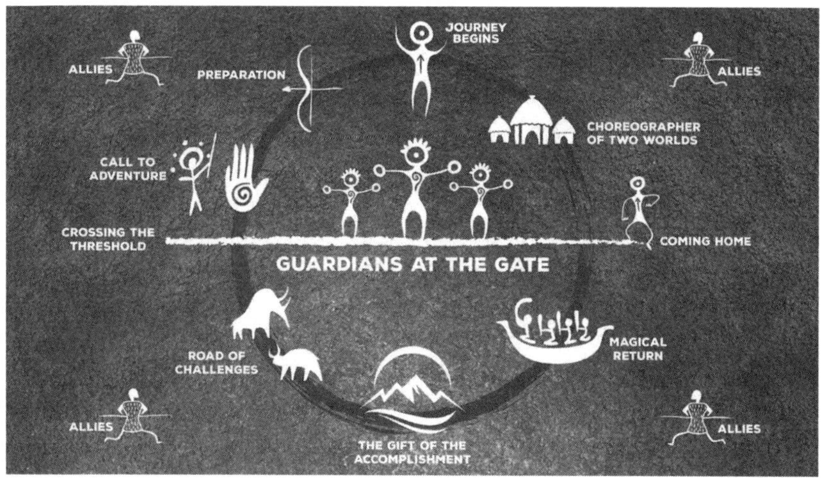

Chapter Twelve

"What I think is that a good life is one hero journey after another. Over and over again, you are called to the realm of adventure, you are called to new horizons. Each time, there is the same problem: Do I dare? And then if you do dare, the dangers are there, and the help also, and the fulfillment and the fiasco. There's always the possibility of a fiasco. But there's always the possibility of bliss."

—JOSEPH CAMPBELL

While I was in graduate school for my Master of Science program in experiential education, a professor exposed me to the work of Joseph Campbell and his concept of the Hero's Journey. He had become famous for his *Power of Myth* documentary of interviews with Bill Moyers, sold in a box set. My professor said he would play the entire series of interviews and then we could discuss the ramifications after each section. He sat in the dark in the back of the class and drank coffee. At first this seemed a questionable way to teach our graduate class. Don't know what to teach? Show a movie.

Throughout the interviews, Campbell described journeys through life that people took throughout ancient mythology and across multiple global cultures. He spoke about choices. He spoke about consequences. He described the ever-present barriers to success and called them "Guardians at the Gate." He revealed Allies that were always available to help us through difficult situations. He cautioned about the difficulty of coming back from big life experiences. He talked about "following your bliss."

My easily distracted mind stopped doodling and flirting with the young woman next to me. I suddenly realized that what he was describing was a map! He showed a way of navigating life through various stages of preparation, challenge, struggle, and accomplishment. I got goose bumps. It was as if I were staring at a dusty treasure map with dotted lines and *X* marking the spot. This was a map for life. No one had ever given me a map to understand life, and this guy in the video was laying it out step-by-step. I looked back at my professor sipping coffee in the dark. He grinned at me and nodded his head.

Like wiping a foggy windshield clear, I could suddenly see where all the things that had happened in my life could be charted around the circle of the Heroic Journey. When I decided to join the trip across Africa for six months at eighteen? That was me answering a Call to Adventure. When I applied and won a grant to study Indonesian for an intensive year at Cornell Grad School? That was me answering a Call to Adventure. When I bought a pickup truck from a cop at night from the Central Park Precinct on 86th Street and drove out of New York, headed for a new life in Minnesota, that was me again answering the Call to Adventure. When my application was rejected at a new TV station called Cable News Network, before it became CNN, that was me slamming into the Guardians at the Gate, the Heroic Journey's version of a roadblock. When I didn't get a job after ten interviews at Citibank, that was me slamming into the Guardians at the Gate again. It all started to make sense. I began to see that everything I had ever done or tried to do could be plotted as a stage somewhere on the Heroic Journey cycle. After reading more of the works of Joseph Campbell, I was convinced that the Heroic Journey held the key to self-awareness and personal empowerment, and I focused on it for my master's thesis.

I realized that if my life could be plotted on the Heroic Journey circle in hindsight, I might be able to use it as a map and navigate life before and while I was going through it.

Every event in my life has made me who I am today; some things made me more compassionate, and I like to say "brought honey to my heart," and others made me stronger and more resilient, giving me "strength to my sword arm." Having adopted this new lens, I was no longer a victim of other people's behavior. My limited self-belief system would no longer cripple me. It was now obvious that, for example, the job that I didn't get in international banking at Citibank, while a devastating blow at the time, would have been a terrible career choice for me.

I wanted to take ownership of my life and not live by default, blaming my mother or my father or God for the life I had. While this mindset shift—this aha moment—was instantaneous, practicing it was going to take time.

I have been trying to live this way ever since. Choice is always there for me. I can wake up and forget all of this, or I can embrace this new way of thinking. By pausing and checking in with myself, I can see where I am on the Heroic Journey and give myself and other people more grace, seeing the good in people and the purpose of events, and claim a much better, more "whole" life, filled with gratitude, wonder, and awe. When we live with the Heroic Journey Mindset, each element on our journey is designed to teach us something. Socrates is purported to have said, "The unexamined life is not worth living." I would proffer my version of his statement, that the unexamined journey is not worth taking.

The more aware we are of the stages of Joseph Campbell's Heroic Journey cycle, the more likely we will reap the benefits of an examined life, a consciously lived life, a richer, more whole and happier life.

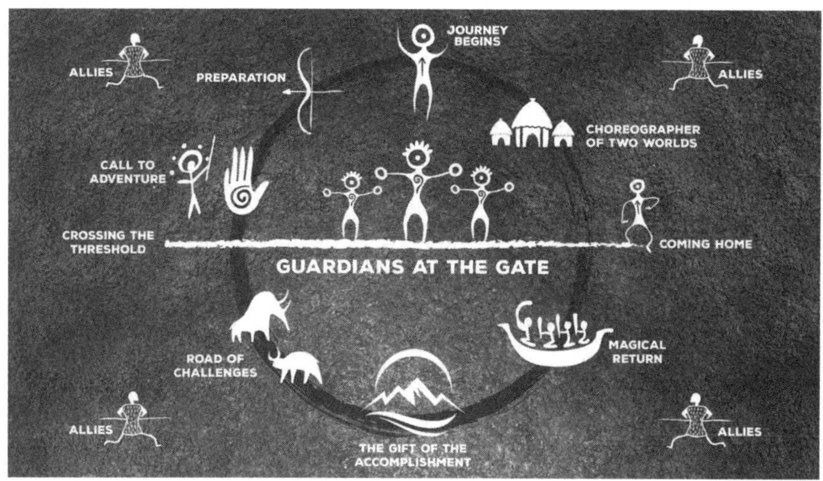

Chapter Thirteen

"The Adventure is always and everywhere a passage beyond the veil of the known into the unknown; the powers that watch at the boundary are dangerous; to deal with them is risky; yet for anyone with competence and courage the danger fades."

–JOSEPH CAMPBELL

The stages of my adapted version of Campbell's Heroic Journey flow counterclockwise (see the graphic above). In this and the following chapters, I'll briefly explain the role each one plays in the circle and then dive deeper into how I've applied it to my life.

The Journey Begins

As every good story begins, we have a point of origin, a place, a time, and a sense of who we are. This can mean both family of origin and the environment around our time of birth, or it can be at whatever point we realize we are on a journey.

In my case, I was born into a loving family suddenly thrust into chaos by my father's aneurysm, with a young, single mother struggling to manage her nursing career, her disabled husband, and two young children, with little emotional support from her parents or in-laws. My journey began with a palpable sense of dread and impending doom, which I took on from the energies I felt in the room. Like a neurotic family dog, I seemed to develop a hypersensitivity to tension and anxiety in my home (and other people's homes, for that matter) and was in a constant state of vigilant stress. For years, I looked at my story of origin as an embarrassment. I was ashamed of how little money we had, of my father's physical state, and of my shame itself. My place of origin, as is the case for many, was complicated and troublesome, and sometimes extravagant. It is from this place that my journey began.

After we moved, attending Harvey, the private boy's school, was another sort of beginning. It took me out of the dangerous realm of climbing and shoplifting and thrust me into the rarefied world of scholarly rigor. As I described, in some ways, I welcomed the change, but in others, I felt newly untethered. We didn't belong to a golf club. We were not landed gentry. In some ways, I did not belong, and I knew it. What developed was an uncanny ability to act, to pretend, and to try to fit in. A chameleon blends into its surroundings as a way to survive; I learned to do the same thing. Again, this set me on a new trajectory, a new journey. I began many journeys throughout my life—first my life as a whole and then all the new beginnings I encountered: traveling abroad, going to college and graduate school, joining AA, moving to New York City, starting new jobs, living overseas, getting married, then divorced . . . over and over I started new phases of my life, for so long unaware of Campbell's helpful framework to understand them, plan for them, and make meaning of both the ups and the downs.

The beginning of anyone's Heroic Journey can be their place of origin, or it can be when they realize they are embarking on one—a point of awareness that this life might actually mean something. They have a purpose to fulfill. Some come to this realization early, while others are struck with it years later, often after a calamity strikes or a change of state shakes them out of their familiar pattern. Once I was shaken out of my own, as the concepts of the Heroic Journey seeped into my soul, I realized that all the limitations and disabilities of my childhood had set me up in more positive ways than I appreciated at the time. The schooling and life experiences—such as dealing with my loving but dysfunctional family, which sent me to years of therapy—actually helped set me on the path toward a compassionate career and gave a gift for building lasting friendships and a portfolio of life experiences that, looking back, I could never have imagined. I turned the adversity into my university, and I learned in hindsight how blessed I was.

In 2006, when TED Talk videos came on the scene, I was stunned by the power and impact of the stories. I watched as many as I could find and shared them with friends, and I still use them in the corporate workshops I lead today. I always wanted to do one but never thought that I could. When I saw a notice in 2017 that my alma mater was hosting a regional TEDx, a smaller-venue version of the same program, I thought I might give it a try. Thus, my TEDx journey began. Attempting to create and deliver the talk—something that I wasn't sure I could do—made me realize that even doing a TED Talk could be seen as a Heroic Journey. With that, I began to plan for all the stages of the circular Journey to unfold ahead of me.

The Preparation

"The better part of valor is discretion, in the which better part I have saved my life."

—William Shakespeare

This stage follows our decision to do any big thing. It is a time of taking stock to determine whether we have what it takes to accomplish this challenge, and, if so, prepare accordingly. If we want to run a 5K race or a marathon, we train, we practice, and we build up our endurance for the challenge.

When I got into rock climbing, I loved the focused exercise of building muscle and seeing the visible gains I was making on a climbing route. When I moved to Bangka Island, off the coast of southern Sumatra, Indonesia, to run a corporate training program for two years, the preparation of bringing my wife and daughter was significant. We needed to find house sitters, prepare the house for leaving, and pack for the overseas assignment. For that adventure, and a later stint working in Japan, I focused on language study so that I would have more dexterity in conversations with colleagues in those countries.

When I decided to take up the sport of polo at the ripe age of fifty-five, I needed to take stock of my physical condition and get some polo gear. The taking-stock stage comprises a physical, mental, emotional, and spiritual assessment of readiness for the challenges ahead. There was much *taking stock* when I decided to deliver the TEDx Talk. First, I had to find out what it took to do one. I asked people I knew who had delivered them, I bought books on the subject, and I watched more TED Talks. Then I set out with a six-month deadline to prepare for this challenge.

These were all events I knew were coming. I assessed the risk and opportunity, made a decision, and paved the way, as best I could, for success.

In contrast, the Preparation stage can also apply to one's readiness for an unknown life, understanding that something is always coming. Often, we do not know what the future holds or how to prepare. That is when we must ready ourselves on multiple fronts: emotional, mental, physical, and spiritual. This is the Preparation that can be the most ambiguous but can also prepare us best for the "liberal arts" of life. I did not have this perspective when I was younger, so there were many challenges I dove into unprepared. I was certainly not prepared for a life lived with a father in long-term care and an alcoholic mother; I was not prepared for my trip across Africa (looking back now, I could have done much more to ready myself for such a grueling trip); and I was not prepared for marriage when I jumped headfirst into that huge commitment. As I said in the introduction, I wish I would have had this book to guide me then.

Now that I have this mindset, I apply it to the rest of life that stretches out before me. I want to prepare; I want to be agile and flexible for whatever is to come.

Any of the paths to wellness—that is, focusing on exercise, good nutrition, healthy sleep rituals, and meditation and yoga—are excellent ways to stay prepared for any eventuality. At different points in my life, I studied aikido, learned some spoken Japanese and Hindi, enrolled in self-actualization workshops, and became certified as a leader of Interplay, an improvisational dance practice. Each of these activities brought me more in touch with my inner state of well-being, and my focus on healthy relationships with other people were an important preparation for the journey ahead.

No matter how well we prepare, we will always falter in some way, but that is where grace comes in. The journey to wholeness need not be a harsh one; it is a nurturing process where we notice everything, evaluate consequences, self-correct, and begin anew. One day, I realized that self-correction was akin to the rumble strips on highways and started noticing when I was going off the road of my life. When my car felt the bumps in the middle or side of the road, I knew I was drifting into danger. If I stopped exercising, watched too many videos, and ate crappy food, I would feel the rumble strips telling me that I was starting to veer off the path I wanted to be on. I would get irritable, overly critical, and defensive as that nagging feeling told me I was going off course. The same was true with other categories, too; for example, if I lost touch with God or my Higher Power, it was painfully obvious. The rumble strips would be deafening and bring me back onto the road.

The Call to Adventure

"An adventure is only an inconvenience rightly considered. An inconvenience is only an adventure wrongly considered."

—G. K. Chesterton

The Calls to Adventure can take many forms. They can be job offers, wedding proposals, or deciding to climb a mountain with friends. These are based on our own choices and volition and are often exciting moments full of promise, a mix of knowns and unknowns, but chances we are willing to take.

Joseph Campbell also referred to "precipitating events," those that are usually not of our own choosing but are thrust upon us by outside forces: being fired from a job, suddenly on the path to divorce, or told by a doctor of an incurable disease. Even natural disasters and global wars can be seen as precipitating events. It is one of the many points where our Heroic Journey Mindset can shift us from seeing something as an inconvenience to something more positive: an adventure.

If we are truly prepared and have buoyancy and flexibility—what I called "loose knees" in the TEDx Talk I did eventually give, titled "Developing Your Heroic Journey Mindset"—we are likely to have more internal and external resources to navigate our way to the best possible outcomes in the face of any precipitating events.

All our lives we are faced with Calls to Adventure. When I was dared to cross the bridge on the outside of the fence, when my mother suggested I graduate high school early and cross Africa instead of bumming around my spring semester of my senior year, when my wife and I chose to face her cancer head-on, those were all Calls to Adventure. For those who have recently retired, their Heroic Journey is about to get interesting. For those who have just found out they are going to have a baby, this is the beginning of a new Heroic Journey they will soon take with their partner and child to be. For those who are recently divorced, the journey begins.

When we pick up the mantle of the "hero," recognizing that each of these challenges will test us, we do something magical. We link to the powers of the ages and people before us who have faced unimaginable challenges and not only survived but thrived. We humble ourselves to ask for help to make good choices, and then we choose or deny the invitation. I can think of many other Calls to Adventure, which I haven't yet mentioned, that I chose to accept:

- Entering a one hundred-mile Adirondack Canoe Classic race with mediocre paddling skills
- Traveling to Indonesia as an American Field Service exchange student at seventeen
- Riding a horse bareback at a rodeo in Lander, Wyoming

- Rock climbing in the Shawangunks and Pingora in the High Peaks Cirque of the Towers region of the Wind Rivers and the Middle and Grand Tetons and Devils Tower in Wyoming
- Getting certified as a bareboat sailing captain so I could charter sailboats and catamarans
- Getting engaged three times to people I never married
- Getting a tattoo
- Buying a new home, three times
- Submitting an essay and winning a *Sail Magazine* contest
- Leading corporate Stretch Expeditions in the Amazon, sailing in the Caribbean, working with artists in Cuba, and hosting a scuba diving trip in Roatan, Honduras
- Committing to learning the art and science of fly-fishing
- Buying and restoring a twenty-one-year-old Porsche Boxster (forest-green metallic!)
- Entering a Sherlock Holmes pastiche writing contest
- Getting SCUBA certified at sixty-four years old
- Writing this book

Each "yes" that I answered to the preceding Calls to Adventure gave me the opportunity to experience something I hadn't up to that point. It cut and polished another facet of the diamond of my life so that I might shine more brightly and encourage others to step up to the challenges they face.

I can also remember a few Calls to Adventure that I did not take—in fact, refused to take:

- Taking LSD and heroin

- Getting accepted to a Master of Divinity program at Union Theological Seminary but withdrawing before I matriculated
- Having an affair while I was still married
- Racing a policeman at a stoplight
- Quitting a job because I was mad at the boss
- Smuggling drugs back from Kenya
- Getting accepted into the Doctor of Education program at University of St. Thomas but withdrawing before I matriculated
- Getting more tattoos
- Drinking or taking drugs again

Each "adventure" that I refused to take has also had consequences, but often not doing something was the better choice at the time.

How I accepted or refused the Calls defines my life and my character. Any success I had with experiences is based on my preparation, mindset, and positive attitudes in the face of challenge and a strong connection to a caring community. And probably due to a good deal of luck.

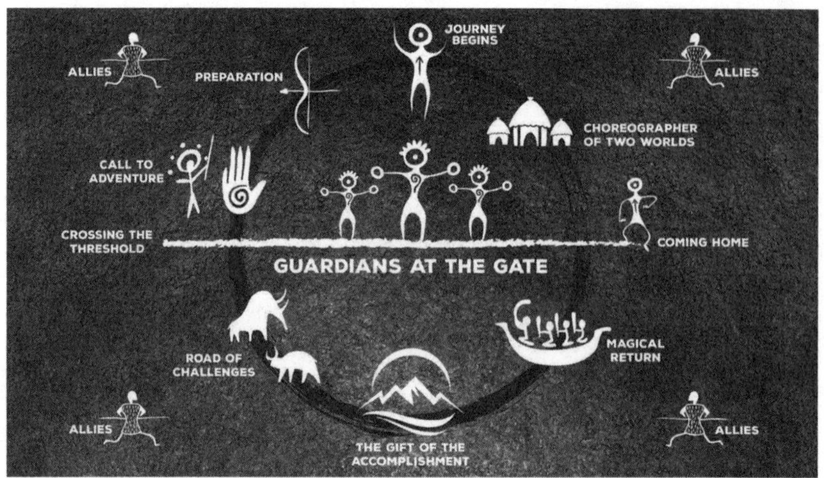

Chapter Fourteen

"This is a brief life, but in its brevity it offers us some splendid moments, some meaningful adventures."

—RUDYARD KIPLING

One of the more powerful aspects of adopting the Heroic Journey model to help us navigate our lives is the concept of Allies. Sometimes disguised, these helpful agents are here to help us at every step of the way. It is our job to look for them and utilize them.

Allies

One of the gifts of the Heroic Journey is that Allies are present throughout the entire process. In the graphic, I have them at each of the four corners as a reminder that they are wonderful resources and often cloaked in a way that we might not see them or appreciate them as Allies. They can help us with mindset and right thinking when we start to go into a downward spiral. Seeking Allies for our Heroic Journey is an important aspect of launching successfully into the unknown. They are an invaluable resource at every step of the way. But we must learn to see them for who they are.

In 1989, as I readied for my move to Minnesota, I bought a 1970s era Ford F-100 pickup truck from a police officer at the Central Park precinct at night (not recommended). I was naive and had no idea of the actual condition of the truck. When the engine died in the McDonald's drive-through at ten at night in a pouring rain, I thought I was sunk. I can still hear the woman's voice through the squawk box, telling me to pull forward. I couldn't. My engine was dead on my "new" old truck. Suddenly, from out of the shadows emerged a guy with a coat over his head who said he would fix the truck for twenty dollars. He jumped the solenoid with a pair of pliers, and I was off and on my way. This Ally was at first unwanted, even feared, when he approached my window in the dark, but I then realized he was an angel in disguise, an unexpected Ally on my journey. He well-earned the twenty bucks.

The Calls to Adventure will be numerous and multifaceted. It is still hard at times to discern whether I should answer or refuse each call. Having mentors or Allies in place has been critical to the success of my journeys. I must be vigilant to leverage them and their experience as I discern the calls I receive. I must continue to develop these relationships for the journey ahead. I learned to seek the wisdom of those I admired and respected. I looked for people who had an appreciation for what I was doing and what it took to do it. In AA, they say, "Stick with the winners." I looked for winners. Invariably, they were willing to help me in my Preparation stage to be ready for the elements that they had also encountered.

I remembered hearing that in the Middle Ages, young boys were sent off from poor farms to learn to be knights. They spent up to nine years away from their families to study and practice the art and science of chivalry, swordsmanship, dance, and equestrian skills. When they returned, they were almost unrecognizable. The boys had grown into young adults, and they had mentors for life. They had relationships with teachers who gave of themselves so that they would grow into their best selves. I started to look for mentors: people who would serve in this role for me.

Guardians at the Gate

"The Adventure is always and everywhere a passage beyond the veil of the known into the unknown; the powers that watch at the boundary are dangerous; to deal with them is risky; yet for anyone with competence and courage the danger fades."

—Joseph Campbell

The Heroic Journey is not often an easy one, and it is fraught with obstacles, some real and some symbolic. Once we hear the Call to Adventure and decide "Yes, I am going to go do this thing!" we sometimes set off naively, as if all is well. What lies ahead, unbeknownst to us, is the first crossing of a threshold, a doorway into the path we have chosen. What we first bump into as we approach this new threshold, this line of demarcation, are the Guardians at the Gate, very real and symbolic blocks to our progress.

I like to think of them as giant sumo wrestlers who are here to push us back. We get close, they push us back; we try again, they push us back. Our tempers might flare, we declare our outrage, or we give up and turn back. The Guardians at the Gate have done their job.

The job of the Guardians is to help us clarify our intentions. Are we really choosing to take this particular fork in the road, or was it a half-hearted idea? How many attempts we make and how strongly we persist is often a good barometer for our resolve. If we give up easily, the sumo wrestlers take a smoke break, as they figure we are just another pesky dilettante. To reap the rewards and treasures of a true Heroic Journey, we need to be up to the task. We must go at this with the determination that we can take on any challenge before us.

The Guardians, curiously enough, are actually helpers in disguise. If we are not prepared, we will not survive the journey. If we are not strong enough and clever enough to get past the Guardians standing in front of the threshold, we are clearly not up to the task.

For example, personal relationships are tested in many ways to see if they are strong enough for a lifelong bond. Countless couples dissolve because painting a room, or moving apartments, or getting a dog, or handling a crisis goes so badly that they realize they are not a good fit and break up. Ah, the Guardians doing their job well. Another ill-advised journey is blocked.

Sometimes the battle with a Guardian indicates that more Preparation is needed. That is a good thing: Turn back, beef up the Preparation, armor up, and then return better equipped to get past the Guardians the next time.

I have learned to "pray for roadblocks" when I have a new idea or project so that I am keenly aware of the Guardians and what they are trying to teach me.

The journeys we are on are happening on many levels, and what we might not see, as we blindly hurtle down a road, is that the bridge is out farther ahead, and the flat tire we curse now is actually saving our lives. The Guardians at the Gate, in some cases, are actually Allies to us, though at the time we might not interpret them that way.

I took up polo, at the overripe age of fifty-five, and I probably should have seen the signs that I had missed my window. It would have been safer to enjoy the sport from the sidelines. But I had long held to the adage that "Ships are safer in harbors, but that is not why ships were built." I had had enough riding lessons over the years to make me think I could do it. I found a good polo school, with a patient Argentinian teacher, and learned the skills and the strategies of the game. While certainly not the best on the team, I played along and even scored the occasion goal. I came off various horses for various reasons five times, and the last one nearly killed me: I got on a horse at a tournament in South Dakota that was not willing to be ridden, and it bucked me up and landed on top of me with such force that it winded me and cracked a couple of ribs. People rushed to help, astounded that I was not more hurt than I was from a throw like that. I limped back home, grateful to be alive, and took it as a clear, if painful, sign from my Guardians at the Gate that I was not to pursue this sport any further. Reluctantly, but gratefully, I listened.

When I decided to try to deliver a TEDx Talk on the Heroic Journey and my wife's cancer journey, it was a Call to Adventure, a crazy idea that I thought probably wouldn't happen: too many hurdles to jump through with the application process, the demo video, and the stiff competition. I had been watching TED Talks since their inception, and I was a little daunted and in awe of the speakers, the sparse stage sets, and the red circle–carpeted platform. I dodged the Guardians that I found in the process of strict deadlines, unanswered phone calls, and ambiguous guidelines of what would be accepted, and I threw myself into doing the best damn demo video I could. And then I turned it over to the God of my understanding. If it was supposed to happen, it would. It was out of my hands. The news came by email.

"We are excited to inform you that your TEDx Talk has been approved. Please contact us to schedule your first preparation meeting."

First reaction: *Wow, cool, I was accepted!* Immediate second reaction: *Yikes, now I have to deliver a TEDx Talk!*

Crossing the Threshold

Crossing the Threshold is a critical turning point. We have gathered our resolve and encountered and bested the Guardians at the Gate, and we are now setting out on a new path toward the journey of our choice. One of the interesting definitions Joseph Campbell has for *threshold* is not just a doorway or sill into a building but rather "the level or point at which you start to experience something, or at which point something starts to happen." Another of Campbell's definitions links to the spiritual elements: "A frontier that cannot be crossed without the heart being passionately engaged and woken up."

These definitions serve us well. When we "cross the threshold," things do start to happen. We could not have dodged the Guardians at the Gate unless we were wholehearted in our conviction; the Guardians actually ensure that. And once we are wholehearted about anything we intend to do, the cosmos has a wonderful way of conspiring on our behalf. It is a secret power that we have, which we often don't discover until years later: the power of wholehearted intention.

Many cultures have symbolized and ritualized the crossing of a significant threshold. Sailors know this point of departure well. There is even a special flag that boats fly when they head out from the safety of their last port: the nautical flag for the letter *P*, "the Blue Peter," a blue flag with a white square. It tells the world that they are "outward bound." There is a reverence to this point where after the hoopla, the cheering, there is a slight chill of sobering realization. Hats are often removed as the ships pass by. We do not know what lies ahead, and some of us may not come back from this trip.

When I crossed the Sahara Desert in 1978, we drove our truck three times around a stone monument to bless our safe passage. Some laughed, some yelled, but the rest of us were silent. We quiet ones knew that this was a prayerful entry into the unknown, the world of uncertainty that lay before us. I felt a chill as I looked at the vast surface of sand stretching south across the continent of Africa.

Another example: Once I got the go-ahead to give a TEDx Talk, I Crossed the Threshold into the "next level." I now had to write out what I would say in a thirteen-minute presentation, pay a talented graphic artist to help me with slides, and ratchet up my public speaking game. The Threshold was not something I was going to easily step over, like a doorway. I saw it more like a rock climbing mantle move, where I reached an edge above me and had to pull myself up with as much grace and finesse as I could muster. This was going to be hard. Really hard. Maybe the most public thing I had ever done. A new Threshold that would require me to perform at another level of my abilities. The exciting thing is that all the roads I had traveled up to this point in my Heroic Journey had brought me to this point. I had all I needed to take on this challenge.

Road of Challenges

"Adversity does not build character, it reveals it."

—James Lane Allen

And so here we are. We have dodged the Guardians, Crossed the Threshold, and are on the road to adventure. This stage is the litmus test of the entire journey. The Road of Challenges is the part when it gets hard, harder, and harder still. Long after the exciting departure, it is the lonely time when we are hungry, angry, lonely, and tired; when we run out of gas on the desert highway, lose our passport, or find ourselves recently divorced in a duplex apartment wondering how we got there. It is at this point in the race when we want to give up.

The Road of Challenges can be daunting. It has beaten better people than you and me, and they have given up and turned back. Mentors or Allies, consulted during this stage, can help us stay in the game and help us process what is happening so we don't give up yet. We need to seek our Allies to help us. In our family, my mother often reminded us, "Don't give up five minutes before the miracle."

Our level of preparation, our spiritual faith, our physical fitness, our capacity to solve problems, our ability to work well with our companions—all of this will be tested. We will surely struggle. We will often fail. We will feel demoralized. We will ache all over. We will doubt ourselves and our leaders. We will wish, at some point, that we hadn't embarked on this journey. Each trial will be a test of our capacity under strain, our ability to find hope when we suffer, and our skills at keeping the flickering flame of our intentions alive despite great odds. The old sailing phrase "attitude is everything" refers to the angle our boat and sails are to the wind, and that is underlying the simple reminder that our attitudes and perspectives in life are critical to our success.

When my wife, Tanya, was diagnosed with throat cancer—a shocker since she was a nonsmoking, nondrinking vegetarian—she found herself at this critical point. A precipitating event had been thrust upon her and a choice presented before her: Shrivel up in a ball and wait for it to be over or step up, lean in, and do all she could to embrace the challenge. She chose the latter, and to take more ownership of this process, even renamed two medical devices the doctors insisted she install: "Power" for the port for blood transfusions and "Purpose" for the PEG feeding tube. Rather than bemoan these two "inconveniences," she renamed them and brought them along as Allies to the cause. She now had Power and Purpose as partners on her journey.

There were many obstacles on the Road of Challenges during my journey through Africa: the food being washed downriver, the heat, the passport situation, and certainly the malaria. Throughout my young life, my mother's addiction, my own, my struggles to stop drinking, my obsession with romantic love and need for validation from others—all of these were obstacles to overcome. I could have been taken down by any one of them, but instead, without knowing at the time that I was on a particular journey, with the help of others and something rather intangible pulling me forward, I overcame them.

The TEDx Talk journey required that I write, develop, rewrite, and memorize the entire piece, all while still doing my job and keeping up responsibilities at home. There were times when I thought it was too hard. I couldn't do it. I didn't want to give up, but I was afraid I wouldn't be good enough. Fear and doubt crept in. I pushed on, stayed with it, and gave it my all. I remember commuting to work, speaking the lines out loud, delivering my talk at sixty-five miles an hour, again and again, until I got it right. I even tested it with some of my corporate groups. I was almost ready.

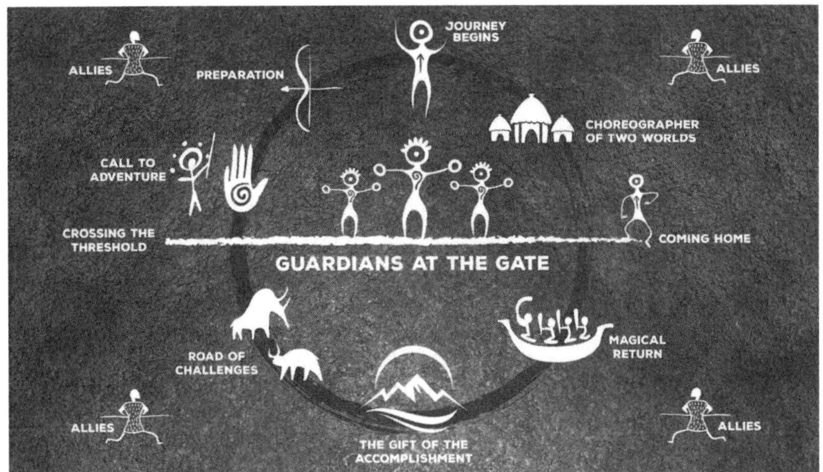

Chapter Fifteen

"A person is a person because of other people."

—AFRICAN PROVERB

The Heroic Journey stages help us pause and name what is happening in our lives. Like Charles Darwin in his audacious pursuit to document every living thing in his tome *On the Origin of Species*, our taxonomy of our life stages makes them more real and calls our attention to what is actually happening so we don't miss anything.

The Gift of the Accomplishment

"Every failure to cope with a life situation must be laid, in the end, to a restriction of consciousness."

—Joseph Campbell

When we do the hard thing—when we stay with it and, despite all circumstances, accomplish what we set out to do, we have reached the summit. We get something that no one else has, that sense of our own capacity and capabilities. We rejoice in our newly found skills, the sense of self that we feel in the core of our being.

Joseph Campbell recognized that the Gifts of the Accomplishment are ours to keep, but they require an increase in awareness. When we see our lives as daily Heroic Journeys unfolding, when we reframe challenges and bring mindset shifts like Power and Purpose to our aid, we can better predict a more positive outcome. I recall as a child seeing a bumper sticker that said: "Life is a bitch, and then you die." I was stunned by that phrase as a worldview, that one could see this passage as simply one of misery until it was over. While that may be the experience some people have, and I have compassion for them, I cannot help feeling that practicing the Heroic Journey Mindset might have lightened their load, attracted more Allies, and given them glimpses of physical and emotional breakthroughs that would have changed their lives for the better.

There are countless stories of amputees, disabled veterans, recovering alcoholics, and people who have faced great calamity who have reframed their blindness, their loss of limbs, their accidents that burned their bodies as gifts that helped them live better lives. They overcame their challenges and not only rose above them but turned them into accomplishments that have taken them places they would never have dreamed of attaining had they not been so afflicted. They inspire me. My friend Erik Weihenmayer, famous for being the first blind person to summit Mt. Everest, would attest to the power of uncovering the belief system that there is more inside you than you know. He and his parents could have given up when the degenerative eye disorder retinoschisis finally took Erik's sight. But it was through their untiring spirit of adventure and willingness to take this seeming calamity and turn it into an adventure that has given Erik more amazing experiences than many of us will ever know.

He has done incredible work on behalf of the organization he cofounded, No Barriers USA, and the Soldiers to Summits project to pass on his enthusiasm for thriving in the face of seemingly insurmountable challenges.

Another person I met, John O'Leary, burned over 90 percent of his body as a nine-year-old and turned that experience into his gift to the world—an encouragement to take on any challenge and harvest the gifts those challenges give us. Argentinian Belen Rodriguez, founder of Minnesota-based Quebracho Empanadas, speaks eloquently in public about her Heroic Journey of launching her award-winning food start-up and then having to shut it down due to economic challenges. Rather than living diminished by this experience, she stands proudly on her team's accomplishments and shares her wisdom and experience with other food start-up groups. Her indefatigable spirit is a beacon of light and hope for entrepreneurs.

In his exhaustive survey of countless cultures, Campbell found that the path of the ritualized Heroic Journey required physical, spiritual, and even metaphysical awareness of the changes we go through in the process. We need to prepare, we need to choose wisely, and we need to be wholehearted in our intention. We will meet with devastating adversity and need help along the way if we want to survive, let alone thrive. The point of accomplishment is not just the success of climbing a mountain or moving to work in another country. It is a deeper one of awareness, new appreciation for who we are, and the realization that we are capable of more than we think. We limit our own capabilities by thinking less of ourselves.

The summit is often this new awareness of how we have previously allowed our own limitations and limited belief systems to curb our prior success. Now, guided by this new understanding, we are more powerfully equipped for subsequent Heroic Journeys that lie ahead.

Allies can help us at this stage of the Journey. We need to seek them out and let them help us. They can save us from self-sabotaging what we most want to accomplish. Upon reflection, we see that we have reached any summit we have achieved largely because Allies were with us every step of the way. We have prepared, made powerful choices, dodged the Guardian barriers to our progress, and accomplished our goals.

We have climbed the proverbial mountain, and we can celebrate that fact. However, the greater accomplishment is in the reflection of what it took for us to climb the mountain and how that deeper awareness will help us going forward. The fact that we tapped into deeper internal resources, that we reached out to Allies, that we found a positive perspective and helped others along the way is the gift of our recovery from cancer, not just the recovery itself. When she bumps into something challenging today, my wife, Tanya, frequently states, "I can do this . . . I had cancer." She can call upon the gifts of all that she had to summon to get through that journey and apply them to every challenge she will face for the rest of her days. It is a reminder of the gift—not that she climbed the seemingly insurmountable mountain of cancer . . . but that she could, when she activated the right mindset.

In the AA program, we celebrate each year that we maintain sobriety. Every month and year is a milestone of recovery, where through the grace of whatever Higher Power we believe in, the wisdom and support of other members of the recovery community, and our own feeble efforts, we have surmounted a life-threatening affliction. The trick here is to own this awareness and fully embody what it has to teach us. I get to ask myself how I can bring my success and sustaining drive of my recovery from addiction to other areas of my life. I get to ask myself how I can practice the principles of the Twelve-Step program in every aspect of my life.

I was backstage in the green room, waiting to deliver my TEDx Talk. I could hear the person out on stage—the rise and fall of her voice. Some of the others were watching her on the flat-screen, others were rereading their notes, and others were pacing. They called my name. I was next. I was standing now by the black curtains next to the stage. We were all silent. I was reminded of being backstage during high school plays. The presenter was almost done. I looked down at my cowboy boots and wondered if they were the best choice of footwear for my first TEDx Talk.

Then it was my turn. I walked onstage. I started at the beginning, and I looked at the faces in the front row. I was telling a passionate story about hope and healing.

It was my family's story.

It was my story.

It was my wife's story.

I saw the red, neon clock numbers, and I brought it all to a close. I walked off the stage to the muffled sound of applause and realized, in my core, that I did it. I did it!

The Magical Return

"He who travels far will often see things
Far removed from what he believed was Truth.
When he talks about it in the fields at home,
He is often accused of lying,
For the obdurate people will not believe
What they do not see and distinctly feel.
Inexperience, I believe,
Will give little credence to my song."

—Hermann Hesse, *The Journey to the East*

And so, we return from the accomplishment—wiser and more aware of what was necessary on a physical, spiritual, and metaphysical level. We are more appreciative of the community of souls that helped us—in fact, without whom we would never have accomplished what we did. The Return is one of the most misunderstood stages of the Journey. We accomplished great things. We are high on our own success. We might even strut around thinking *look how badass I am*. There should be parades and a commendation medal. But no.

We begin the proverbial down climb to the base camp of our lives. But the Journey is not over; we are but halfway around the circle. More challenges are ahead, and it is the foolhardy and naive who celebrate too soon.

When I co-led a group of novice climbers up to the top of Devils Tower in Wyoming, they celebrated and high-fived each other when they had all finally clambered up. I was more serious and less celebratory. I knew we were only halfway through the adventure. We had to now get everyone back down off the stone monolith safely, and the potential for injury, with our tired crew, made it even more challenging.

[Top of Devils Tower in Wyoming, author crouched in the center.]

This is the time to watch our steps and descend carefully, carrying the riches of accomplishment while also staying alert for new dangers. Wise Allies can help us here, tempering our self-congratulatory enthusiasm as we come back down from the mountain. Stories of the down climb, the expat return, the return to the neighborhood or office after divorce are rife with how unexpectedly difficult it can be. Rather than being celebrated, we sometimes feel a chilly distance between friends; instead of a parade we find ourselves alone in an apartment with a stack of unpaid bills.

Allies can remind us here that the Heroic Journey is not just about the external accomplishments but also the internal awareness of our own gifts, power, perspective, and capabilities. Attaining the summit was where we saw those manifested. The Return is where we must internalize the knowing and own it forever, or we are at risk of losing one of the many life lessons available.

So we return to an "inexperienced" family and public. No one will truly appreciate what we have undertaken and accomplished. Not really. The loneliness we feel is the realization that we are alone in our victory; moreover, we are often painfully alone in our Return.

But all is not lost. This is *our* journey, and while there are public aspects, the owning and our metamorphosis are personal.

I use the word *metamorphosis* intentionally because it captures so much of what is going on. *The Oxford English Dictionary* defines it as: "a change of the form or nature of a thing or person into a completely different one, by natural or supernatural means." That is truly what we are experiencing—a complete metamorphosis of who we are and what we believed to be true into the new being we are becoming now. But it is tricky. We are in grave danger of slipping back into what we were comfortably before. The old us was familiar. We lived it for many years. We know that state of being like the smell of our warm, unwashed sleeping bag; it may be grubby, but it is ours. And, as we will see, the world receiving us back, in many ways, does not want us to change. In fact, many will find our new awareness, attitudes, stated boundaries, and newfound voices to be threatening to them.

When I returned from Africa, I was thoroughly exhausted. We had to push the truck every morning to jump-start it. Our food stores had run so low, we were down to only cooked cabbage and black tea. I had suffered malaria and dysentery, traveled through a cholera outbreak, lost fifteen pounds, and suffered a barely healing tropical ulcer. I was also exuberantly excited with the accomplishment of what had just transpired. It was the trip of a lifetime!

Attending my freshman year at St. Lawrence University, I was coming in hot from the heart of Africa, and all my fellow students looked squeaky clean. One of the many challenges of my Return was to somehow keep fresh everything I had just learned about myself and not revert back to my previous self and pretend it didn't happen.

Pandora's box had opened. I had activated my feral Mowgli self, and he did not want to be put back in the box. In seeking Allies on campus, I connected with my anthropology professor, Dr. John Barthelme, who had worked with Richard Leakey at Lake Turkana. He knew what living in the bush of Africa was like. I spent many countless afternoons and evenings with John and his partner, Sue, helping to process what I had just experienced.

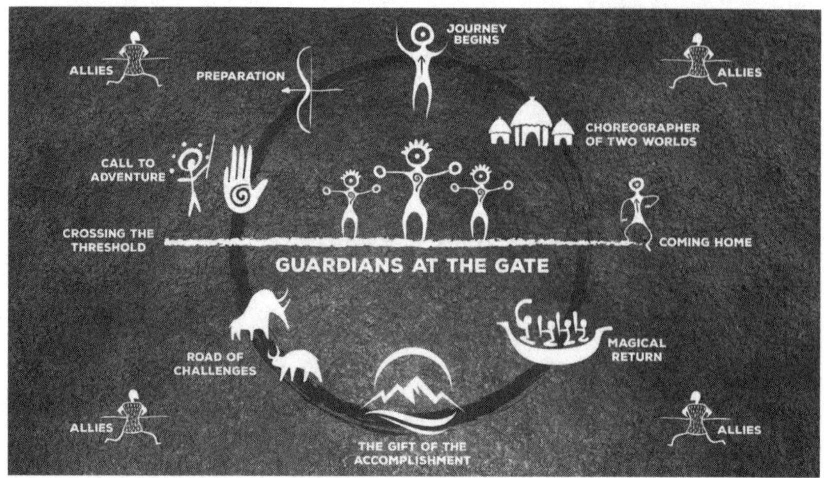

Chapter Sixteen

"Let yourself be silently drawn by the strange pull of what you really love. It will not lead you astray."

—RUMI

As our lives unfurl, as we step around the cycles of life again and again, we are frequently confronted with situations, problems, and roadblocks that we have encountered before. Our humanness is inclined to default to frustration or condemnation, but our burgeoning wisdom has a different perspective. It guides us to see these repetitive situations as an opportunity for us to have another go at solving the puzzle. The Guardians at the Gate, who we encountered as we set out on our Heroic Journey, are waiting for us like smokers in the parking lot behind the movie theater, ready to give us a hard time again. But wait, we have learned important lessons on our Heroic Journey that we can apply to handle the Guardians differently this time. Game on!

The Guardians, Again

As we come around the circle of the Heroic Journey and complete another cycle, aware now of the fragility of our newfound self-awareness, we don't have an easy glide home. Instead, we run into those damned Guardians at the Gate again. This time, they are ready for us. They know they were bested by us before, and they intend to teach us a lesson this time. The lesson is an important one. They say things like: "What have you learned from your Journey such that you can embody it and never forget it?" or in short: "Sit down and shut up. You know nothing!"

To beat the Guardians at the Gate this time, we need to prove that we have internalized all we have learned on the Journey thus far. We must own the internal victory of a new way of thinking, acting, and believing so that we will have an unshakable resolve to remain changed when we get back home. They thrust, they jab, they pounce, they toss us back. This can be daunting, even deflating, upon the heels of our victory. However, when we muster ourselves and admit that they are right, we are able to stand tall in our fullness as the new humbled warrior we are, not the same brittle, defensive person we were before.

Our Guardians at the Gate have actually been our Allies all along. They have helped steer us away from foolhardy endeavors, maybe even when we most wanted to pursue them. They have coached us into techniques so that we could beat the Guardians on the first pass, and they can help us beat them on our second pass by reminding us what is most important about the Journey. It was truly not about climbing the mountain but about climbing out of our inability to climb the mountain before. These Allies are going to help us reenter our lives with fewer bumps and scrapes. Let's use them.

Choreographer of Two Worlds

Reentry from life-changing experiences can be a strange and painful time. On one hand, we have the new way of thinking, and yet on the other, we are faced with all the systems and people in place to reinsert us in our lives exactly how we left it. We need to learn to navigate, deftly, this tricky predicament by being what Joseph Campbell calls a Choreographer of Two Worlds. We don't want to come off high and mighty from our adventures, and yet we also don't want to slip back into our old comfortable behaviors.

And here is another twist: People would generally prefer that we not change too much around them. It makes them uncomfortable. It shows how much *they* are not evolving. So, the Choreographer of Two Worlds stage presents us with the challenge of keeping our new selves in our *old-world* surroundings. We must find a way to live in both worlds until they can integrate into our new, authentic way of being. And that can be bumpy. Remember, reentry sucks. Fasten your seat belt, put on your oxygen mask first, and prepare for a potentially rough landing.

When I worked as an executive director for an Indonesian company on Bangka Island, off the coast of southern Sumatra, I was treated like a king. The company provided a cook, a driver, a nanny, a gardener, and a guard. We lived in the biggest house on the community square. I was recognized as a VIP at the local resort hotel and invited to special gatherings reserved for bank presidents and other business leaders. I spoke Bahasa every day and made friends with many of the staff for life. My time at Bangka Island Outdoors is one of the peak experiences of my life.

My reentry from working at Bangka Island Outdoors in Indonesia was, needless to say, difficult.

I liked being treated like a king. I loved our home on the Taman Sari block. I had gotten quite comfortable with the expat lifestyle. I had become immersed in a culture of amazing people—not as a tourist but as a member of the community. When I returned, I had none of that. I found that my first marriage was disintegrating. I had no job and had two children under four years of age. I had led an international training division in Indonesia, with forty staff and a gorgeous three-hundred-acre property on the beaches of the South China Sea. Now, I had absolutely no status. Nobody cared who I was.

I returned home from a tropical paradise to St. Paul, Minnesota, in the dead of winter. My shipment of teak furniture all cracked in the frozen dryness of February. The crack of one long coffee table sounded like a rifle shot as it split down the middle. Welcome home! I saw the symbolism of the crack in the table as a similar crack in the core of my being. I was a new person, not able to fit into the old shell of who I had been. The loud crack was a wake-up call to a new life and a new world. I needed to own that whole Indonesia experience and bring back to my life in Minnesota all the riches of what I had learned. I needed to step up to yet another challenge and come home and keep the new person I had become.

I sought out other people who had lived and worked overseas. They encouraged me to ask good questions of those I had left home about their experiences in the interim. What had happened to them while I was gone? (Keeping others in mind is one of the ways we can ease back in with less obvious focus on ourselves as the only people who have been through change. Expats and veteran spouses are good examples of people who are often missed in the blur of the journey and yet have had to contend with their own important Heroic Journeys.)

Years ago, Craig Neal from the Center for Purposeful Leadership and I cofacilitated a men's wilderness retreat in the Boundary Waters between Northern Minnesota and Canada. We canoed and portaged our gear into the backcountry for eight days with six men who were hungry for self-reflection and transformation. The night before we packed out was symbolic. From the peace and serenity of the beautiful backcountry we were returning to our lives, with all the craziness waiting to pounce on each of us. Craig, in his wise, grounded way, invited us to hold the power of the trip for as long as we could. He talked about the dangers of slipping back into our old ways.

"When you return, hold your stories close. Don't spill your guts to everyone about what happened for you out here. Share how good you are feeling, but keep your stories close. Also, don't wash your grubby camping clothes right away. Keep the smoky campfire clothes as a reminder of the you that you discovered out here."

Meeting with the Mentor/the Fire Circle

Joseph Campbell relates his version of the Heroic Journey with more stages than I have included. Many of his are due to his mythological references, like Atonement with the Father and the Meeting with the Goddess and the Apotheosis. These may happen for you in your own way. The Heroic Journey is a multilevel chess game happening in its own time and space and is not necessarily as linear as it is portrayed. One additional theme I did want to touch on that has been important for me is his phrase "Meeting with the Mentor."

Ever since seeing the Disney film about Pinocchio and Jiminy Cricket as a child, I was aware of the voices for good that sat hovering over my shoulders. Whether I listened to them or not, I couldn't deny that they were there. I am sure my Jiminy Cricket or God was screaming his head off the day I crossed on the outside of the bridge.

Many times, I chose not to listen, but I was always aware he existed. This image actually gave me my first sense of a mentor, or a wise elder, whom I wanted to add to my life; my father's situation being what it was, I sought other places for support. Seeking mentors became its own mini Heroic Journey for me as I sought to fill the gap of a strong father figure in my life.

I looked for these mentors in male teachers, therapists, neighbors, friends of the family, and Twelve-Step sponsors. Some didn't fit the bill, while others were significant in helping me on my journey. I usually focused on men, since my relationship with women was so distorted that I often confused intimacy with sexuality, but there were many women who also served as mentors in my life.

As I grew older, something significant began to happen. I started being drawn to small groups of men who would gather and talk about life and the living of it. Some of this was ignited by the work of Robert Bly and Coleman Barks and the men's movement in the '80s. I read works by John Bradshaw, James Hillman, Robert A. Johnson, Richard Bach, Samuel Osherson. It certainly made sense anthropologically. First, we start out as boys hanging out with boys, vying to be the king of the hill, running, jumping, and competing in sports. Then, the pursuit of women comes in, trying to find the perfect mate. And then we return to seeking the company of men. By this time, we have let go of the competition and comparisons and now seek the friendship and mutual mentorship of what I call the Fire Circle. The Fire Circle, for me, is a safe gathering where we come together to connect, be vulnerable, share our life stories, and listen and learn from each other. Many women follow a similar path and seek their own Fire Circles with other women later in life too.

[Fire Circles, photo credit David McLain/Caringbridge.]

For me, the Fire Circle was part of the ritual of coming home, the completion of the Journey—the sharing of stories and what we learned from them. When I came back from the Africa trip, the search began for people who had had similar experiences. World travelers seek other world travelers to relive the feelings of what they experienced. Friends who are veterans of the wars in Vietnam, Iraq, and Afghanistan speak of the same pursuit of affiliation. We need to be around people who have seen what we have seen. Twelve-Step recovery groups offer a type of Fire Circle: a safe place to come in from the cold and hear stories of hardship, challenge, and accomplishment. I can grab a cookie and a coffee and sit next to a stranger who is closer to me due to shared experience than I would have thought by looking at him. In each case, we have survived a Heroic Journey and done something hard. We have come back to tell it. I can learn from these people's example how to quiet my demons, bring reality back after my flashes of PTSD, and take things one day at a time, even one hour at a time.

In these Fire Circles, sometimes there was an obvious group leader, but often not. We would co-mentor each other by simply witnessing each other in the process of assembling the jigsaw puzzles of our lives. These men's realizations helped me, and hopefully some of my realizations helped them. During the years that Tanya was undergoing chemo and radiation treatments, I held two Fire Circles to reach out to others to learn what they did in times of stress, fear, doubt, and grief. We talked, we listened, and we learned. It linked us to the thousands of years of lives and the thousands of Fire Circles across the ages and cultures that brought people together to convene a conversation. It healed an inner wound of mine by just showing up, sitting in the circle, and staring into the embers of my life.

Aging is a remarkable Heroic Journey in itself. It requires courage to see our bodies start to break down from hard usage: failing eyesight, diminished hearing, arthritis in my climbing hands, withering muscles, and the sense that the sand in my hourglass may be slipping through, seemingly faster as time goes on. Years ago, I heard the analogy that life is like a diminishing toilet paper roll. My "roll" in life does seem to be shrinking, and each paper sheet seems to hold more value than when it was an overstuffed roll, easily wasted. Rather than watch this process alone, isolated and lonely, I seek the companionship of men who are also in this stage of their lives. They are thoughtful. They are wise. Some are angry or heartbroken at the state of the world. Others are more accepting of the circumstances beyond our control. As we Return, we are Allies to each other. We share what we have learned, where we fell down, how we picked ourselves up. We laugh, we cry, and we keep on keeping on. And always, we come back to the fire. An ancient convenor, fire has been a critical element of survival since it was first discovered. Of course, even today, it still has an important place in our lives. I come back to the Fire Circle: the centering fire, the grounding fire, watching the flickering embers of my past blast heat into the present and slowly gray into shifting coals of gratitude. I am finding that a comforting peace is beginning to replace the restlessness I have felt for years.

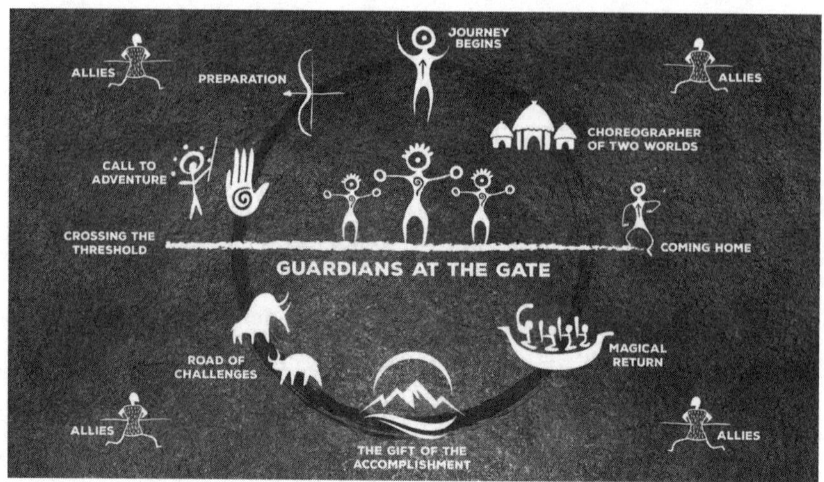

Chapter Seventeen

"It is something out of his own unique potentiality for experience, something that never has been and never could have been experienced by anyone else."
—JOSEPH CAMPBELL

The Heroic Journey has come full circle. We assess what we have done, where we have been, what we have learned. Our busy lives seem to urge us forward onto the next adventure, but we will be better served if we find time to pause, take stock of our present state, and celebrate the completion of one Journey before we take on the next.

Beginning Anew

That is the Journey cycle. Full circle. We prepare, we answer the call of a challenge, we confront Guardians who push us back, we forge on anyway and then slay the dragon or win the princess's hand in marriage. We laugh, we cry, we dance, we bleed. We live. Goddamn it, we live!

And then we come home and try to be better prepared to reenter the circle the next time with more wisdom, humor, curiosity, and gratitude on the next round.

Now we understand the power of the circle of the Heroic Journey and the invaluable aid provided by Allies when we seek them out. On our Journey, we have tapped into our physical ability, intellectual rigor, emotional tool kit, and even called on spiritual and metaphysical entities to help us at our darkest points. And what's more, we better understand *how* to live.

When Tanya invited Power and Purpose to be her companions on her medical journey, she learned she could do that again anytime she needed them. The Heroic Journey, once lived, becomes a mindset, a way of living that humbly invites others to go through the hard things in our lives with us. We now have the tools to see further down the path and a better understanding of what might lie ahead and how we can prepare for surprises, eventualities, and inevitabilities.

There will be other Calls to Adventure—many of them. Some we will choose, some we will refuse. Some events will be precipitating events that throw us once again into challenging experiences. There will be Guardians at the Gate, and now we know them and can give them a wink or a kick as we stride by flashing our VIP badges. These terms will be a part of our new lexicon. We will recognize flat tires and difficult bosses to be the Guardians at the Gate. They might turn us back, or we might laugh to ourselves and navigate forward. There will be many, many Roads of Challenges before us, and we will be ready for them. We will pack food. We will bring our sense of humor. We will humbly ask for help from Allies and spiritual guides, and as my friend David McNally says, "We will not only survive, we will thrive."

As I mentioned at the beginning of this book, we are often on more than one Heroic Journey at a time; the Heroic Journey is never complete. As soon as we Return, there is another one waiting to begin, or we are on two or three simultaneously. I have a Heroic Journey with my wife, Tanya. I have another one with my daughter, Sydney, and my son, Jackson. I have a professional career journey, a self-awareness journey, a recovery journey, a work journey, an aging journey, and even a journey in writing this book.

Once we complete one cycle, it gets easier and easier. We thrash less. We breathe and sleep better. We surrender sooner and are vulnerable when we need to be and can admit we don't know what to do next.

If we do this well, as a gift of graduation, we get to be Allies to others. We have earned the right to be a part of other people's journeys, as you may already be. But naming and claiming your role now brings more responsibility. We get to help people discern the right Calls to Adventure for them, posing questions that help them unlock their inner truths. We get to share stories of our battles with Guardians and how our experience might help others. We get to invite them to bring more humor and humility. We get to witness brave and courageous journeys that will inspire us. And we can be there to help them on the Return, so that their reentries go just a bit more smoothly. It is a noble task and a glorious opportunity to serve others as we have been helped.

As Matthew (10:8) in the King James Bible states, "Freely you have received, freely give."

And we, too, get to begin again. Ideally, this time with a much better sense of who we are, what tools we have, and how capable we are. We stand just a little bit taller. We are a little lighter in our step;

we actually, dare I say, enjoy the journey a little bit more. Yes, even the hard ones.

Reframing My Story

We take a deep breath. We shake off everything that is part of the old narrative, and we breathe into the new narrative. One of my mentors and former sponsor John Rathbun used to always say, "We are where we want to be, or we wouldn't be here."

While sometimes difficult to accept, I get what he is saying. Own our choices. Own our lives. In fact, celebrate that we are exactly where we are supposed to be at this time. All the billiard ball clicks and clacks, all the people, experiences, countries, and emotions, have created the rare work that is each of us. Truly, would we want it any other way?

To reframe our gifts, we must see with new eyes of appreciation. When I learned Interplay Dance, my teachers spoke of watching dancers with "soft eyes" rather than the harsh critical eye of perfection. As I look at myself with soft eyes, I see a deeply compassionate person, caring for the fate of individuals and the state of the world and the environment. Where did that gift come from? Was it a direct result of being raised by a single parent with a disabled father? Maybe. Did being the shortest kid in seventh grade give me an allegiance to the underdogs of the world and a desire to stand up for them? Probably. Did my early exposure to sex and romance put me in contact with truly wonderful people who have made my life richer for the times we spent together? Definitely. Did my travels and deep interactions with cultures and people in over fifty countries, despite encounters with malaria, tropical ulcers, and dangerous situations, help me have a better worldview and perspective for the complexities of the human condition? Absolutely. Each aspect of the painful and dark times in my life birthed a new learning, an awareness like the smelting of gold, burning the dross off the top to purify my heart and give me an undeniably rich experience here on earth.

When I think back on the scene when I had to kill the kittens, paint the attic apartment stairs, or wait hours after wrestling practice, I can now see how each experience added another facet to who I am and how these situations impacted and created the person I am today.

The boy who started drinking and drugging at thirteen stopped drinking at twenty-two and is now forty-two years sober as of this writing. Reframing our gifts is giving credit where credit is due. Kenny Chesney sings about learning how to build a better boat; that is what I am trying to do.

Having had years of therapy, I have learned to take some of the changes into my own hands. When I have come to the end of the road on a particular vice, bad habit, or behavior I want to stop, I do this, and it works:

I thump myself in the chest three times, solidly, and say loudly:

"DONE WITH THAT."

If I am truly done, it works. It is symbolic and declarative. Reframing my gifts means I get to rewire what makes me tick. To get rid of my hiccups, I taught myself at an early age that all I needed was a tablespoon of vinegar. I get to create my own "life hacks" to make my life better.

The language I use is important. It defines my experience. Today, when I have a heavy travel work week, with all the signs that this could be really hard, my former self would have called it Hell Week. And I would have kicked and wrestled my way through it, telling everyone who would listen how hard it was. Today, thanks to my friend David Moriah, instead of calling it "Hell Week," I rename it "Glory Week."

It is a week when I can show what I can do and that I can step up and face my challenges with balanced power.

I had the opportunity once to have a conversation with Jon Kabat-Zinn, the great mindfulness advocate. He was the guest speaker at the Earl E. Bakken Center for Spirituality and Healing at the University of Minnesota for a few days, and because of Tanya's connection to that department, I happened to sit next to him during lunch. His agenda was packed with meetings all week. I asked him how he did it, how he found rest amid such a busy agenda. He quietly chewed his mouthful of food before speaking and said something I have never forgotten.

He said: "I rest all the time."

Boom. Mic drop. Since then, I have practiced it myself. On wildly overbooked days, I pause, call upon the practical wisdom of Jon Kabat-Zinn, and rest. All the time. I meditate in an Uber from airports to hotels. I buy old classic books like *Moby Dick* and read passages of power and beauty. I am learning to rest all the time, so I have sustainable, focused energy to do whatever I need to do. It works. Thank you, Jon!

So, we come to the final act. The curtain is about to draw closed on my mother's life. All she is and was, as it is for all of us, remains in what we leave behind. Her breathing more ragged, halting. My sister and I sit closer and hold her hands. The memories we were chatting about hours ago become internal images for us both. The videos of a lifetime of Oscar-worthy moments—the comedies, the tragedies, the painful and the poignant—blend into a montage of her and our experiences with her. I get to reframe every difficult scene to squeeze out the life juice that shaped who I am, this moment, today. The credits begin to roll, and we realize that she has breathed for the last time. We are her legacy, and the slow rolling credits indicate all that went into the production of a beautiful, complicated, creative woman who faced the challenges of her life the best she could.

The saga of family love and dysfunction doesn't disappear. However, over time, it seems to soften to a watercolor wash of forgiveness that comes over me as I think of the events of which I wrote. Scenes that were harsh and painful and damaging in my early life seem to fade out as though sunlight bleached the colors. I can still make them out, and she is not blameless—none of us are—but the heat of the burn has cooled. What has filled the places of emotional scarring is the tenderness of knowing that we are all human, doing the best we can with the abilities we have at the time. And in reframing the damage, the hurts and little pains, I can turn them like soil into a garden to grow better flowers. What were once weeds, poison ivy, nettles, and burrs that pestered in clothing can now be Block Island beach roses—*rosa rugosa*, fragrant and ever blooming. The work is happening. The healing is replacing the hurting.

PART FOUR:

THE HEROIC JOURNEY GUIDEBOOK

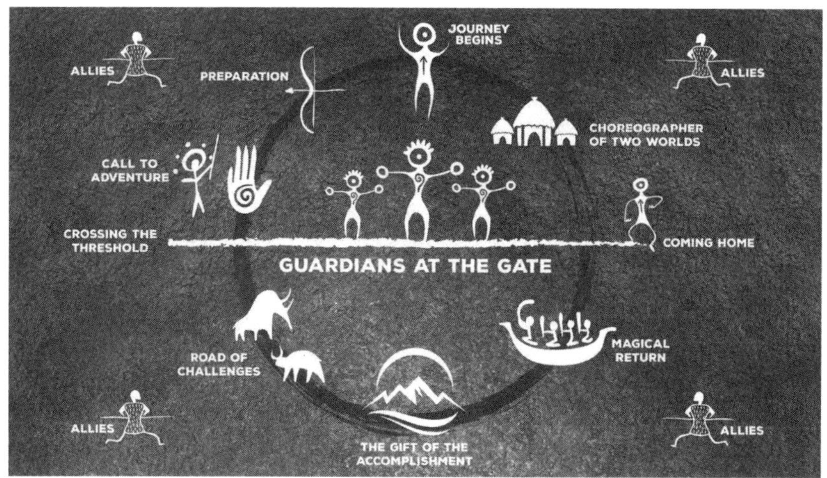

Chapter Eighteen

"Come, come, whoever you are.
Wanderers, worshippers, lovers of leaving, it doesn't matter.
Ours is not a caravan of despair.
Come, even if you have broken your vow a thousand times,
Come, come, come yet again."

—JELALUDDIN RUMI

And now, it's your turn. What stories are you dragging along behind you, like Captain Mendoza, played by Robert De Niro, in *The Mission*? What moments in your past have you allowed to steal your spirit and curb your creativity? They say the best time to plant a tree is twenty years ago. The second-best time is to plant right now.

Guidebook Format

This guidebook is meant to help you apply the Heroic Journey model to your own life. I have walked others through this material countless times, from a group of men gathered around a fire to the leadership teams of Fortune 500 companies, in conference rooms to wilderness adventures in the middle of the North Woods. And now I offer it to a broader audience, to be done wherever, whenever. I have found these questions and activities instrumental in helping both men and women, young and old, find ways to symbolize and reframe their past experiences, prepare for future Journeys, and understand that we are each the hero of our own Journeys. Let's plan accordingly!

In the chapters ahead, each stage of the Heroic Journey is explored using a consistent format—offering a clear description, followed by deeper reflection to help you find personal relevance. Most of the questions and activities focus on future Journeys: how to choose wisely, how to prepare, how to meet challenges, etc. But first, it's important to take a look back at the life you've lived up to this moment. As I discussed in Part Three, reframing my past experiences helped me gain a sense of peace about my life—both the difficult times and the joyous occasions. When I owned and accepted all that had occurred, every billiard ball click against people and experiences, and understood that without those experiences, I wouldn't be the person I am today, I moved toward wholeness. It has changed my life. So before we begin talking about how to best meet the challenges before you, I recommend thinking through your own life experiences and seeing if you, too, can reframe them as parts of your Heroic Journey. If you can identify how your past has defined your present, you will find more peace in that place.

Reframe Acronym

To help with this process, I've developed a helpful acronym to reframe past challenges and hardships and view them as experiences that have helped me grow and adapt, to, as I have mentioned, bring "honey to my heart and strength to my sword arm."

Reframe Model

- **R**eview what actually happened.
- **E**valuate the situation and **E**xtract the silver lining that resulted from the event.
- **F**ind the positive and **F**orgive* the people involved.
- **R**emember you are who you are because of everything that has happened to you.
- **A**ccept everything that has sculpted you: the good, the bad, the challenging.
- **M**ake a conscious effort to own who you are today.
- **E**mbrace your spirit and shine your light brighter for your life experiences.

*A note on forgiveness: There may be situations, actions, and wrongs for which one is unable or unwilling to forgive. To anyone struggling with this, I would ask that you accept that this may take time. You can begin the recovery process by releasing the negative energy and charge that you have with the person or situation such that the impact on you diminishes as you give it less power. This is brave, courageous work. Be gentle with yourself. Trust the process.

Once you've looked back, it's time to look ahead, at your future path—all the Heroic Journeys you'll encounter ahead—and apply the

Heroic Journey Mindset. In my TEDx Talk, I highlight key takeaways that help me daily.

Key Skills to Develop Your Heroic Journey Mindset

1. Keep breathing and develop "loose knees."
2. Trust, have faith, intuit, feel, reflect, and notice everything.
3. Develop an attitude of sacred gratitude.
4. Create a community and symbolize milestones.
5. Unleash your sense of humor.
6. Help others on the path. Pass on what you learn.

What to Expect

The following pages offer ways to apply the Heroic Journey Mindset to your own adventures. Each chapter will have a similar structure:

1. **Summary:** This section reminds you of the key elements of the Heroic Journey stage. At times, I share personal stories to help spark ideas of reflections on your own experiences.
2. **Questions:** This section includes reflection questions and discussion prompts you can use in groups to consider how to apply the Heroic Journey Mindset to your own life.
3. **Activities:** This section offers constructive activities to help you make the most of your current or future Heroic Journeys.
4. **Notes:** Use this space to jot down your notes, observations, and insights.

I hope that the reflection and introspection you'll do in these exercises will give you the same peace and strength I found by applying the Heroic Journey Mindset to my own life. May this help you move forward in courage, my friend. Let's jump in . . .

The Journey Begins

"Breakthroughs come when people learn how to take the time to stop and examine their assumptions."

—Peter M. Senge, *Presence*

Summary

The beginning of anyone's Heroic Journey can be their place of origin, or it can be when they realize they are embarking on one—a point of awareness that this life might actually mean something.

We begin the Heroic Journey the moment we know we are on one. And, if we can identify a purpose for our Journey, it will help serve as an immune system for getting us through difficulties and low points we encounter along the way.

This awareness becomes a significant "point of origin" from which we can begin to ask ourselves questions and move forward with more purpose and intention. However, often when a new Journey begins, it's easy to lose our sense of direction and purpose. We sometimes put our previous experiences in a box and leave them behind. If we don't figure out how to share our past experiences, we are at risk of internalizing our thoughts and feelings, which can be isolating, potentially unhealthy, and, at the very least, limit the integration of the learning from our last experience into our current situation. We need to learn to navigate through this stage. An important element is simply realizing that we are at the beginning of a Journey and that new horizons and new learnings await us, and our experiences can help others go on their own Journeys and discover what horizons and learnings await them.

Whenever we begin a Heroic Journey, we get a chance to improve on our last Journey. We get to learn lessons about our own attitudes and behaviors, and we get to try again at building relationships. When we set out on a Heroic Journey, it helps when we intentionally set out a purpose for the Journey. Granted, another purpose or why may become clearer along the way, but if we identify a purpose for ourselves, we are more likely to look for confirmation from the cosmos that we are on the right track.

The word purpose, to some, may have overwhelming connotations, or it may seem obvious to pick "surviving cancer" and ask you to "find the purpose in it." It is important to unpack it a bit to be totally clear on our intentions.

Sometimes, the struggle of what is happening right in front of us can be all-consuming and distract us from thinking about the bigger scheme of things. However, this is an important life skill to reinforce—finding a way to balance living in the present with nurturing a long-term perspective and a Heroic Journey framework for life.

Viktor Frankl, in *Man's Search for Meaning*, wrote the following about his time surviving the concentration camps:

"When we are no longer able to change a situation, we are challenged to change ourselves."

"Everything can be taken from a person but one thing: the last of the human freedoms—to choose one's attitude in any given set of circumstances is to choose one's own way."[3]

---

3 Viktor Frankl, *Man's Search for Meaning* (Beacon Press, 2006).

By determining a vision or purpose and understanding the why of your Journey, you can take attitudinal control to get through even the worst of situations. In less dramatic circumstances, it can allow for more fun and help bring recognition of small victories each day.

Richard Leider, acclaimed speaker and noted author of many books on purpose, including *Claiming Your Place by the Fire*, encourages drafting a purpose statement that you can use to guide you in your choices.

Based on his guidance, I drafted a purpose statement early in my career:

"I will seek to always break the **ICE.**"

- **I**nspire an awareness of people's innate abilities.
- **C**hallenge them to creative action.
- **E**ncourage learning via reflection.

This purpose statement has guided me for over thirty-five years.

Questions

- At Outward Bound, we say that "your course begins the moment you know you are going on it." The Journey has begun. How can you celebrate this?
- What can you do to make this beginning even better than your last?
- How can having a sense of purpose or why help you embark on this experience?
- What do the words *purpose* and *why* mean to you? What other words work for you?
- Richard Leider is a friend and subject-matter expert on the topic of purpose. He has devoted his life to helping people

clarify and live by their purpose. In his book *Claiming Your Place by the Fire*, he says it is "not so much a matter of *finding* a purpose that gives us such true joy as it is a matter of *recognizing* what our purpose already is and *claiming* it."[4]

- How might this Journey or new connection with others serve to help you in life?
- While it is important to think and feel what our purpose might be, it can be really helpful to share those thoughts and feelings with others. With whom can you share this?

Activities

1. Take time to identify for yourself what your purpose or why is for taking this Journey and create a statement of purpose.

Examples of Statements of Purpose as You Begin Your Heroic Journey:

- "Today I am going to stay sober and not take a drink."
- "Today I am going to find someone who is having a harder time than me and help them have a better day."
- "Today I am going to climb this crazy mountain to prove to myself that I can do it."
- "I am going to move beyond the feelings I have about this divorce and get on with my life."
- "While losing this job was depressing, I am going to rally and see it as a launching of a new kind of work that I want to do."

4 Richard Leider, *Claiming Your Place by the Fire: Living the Second Half of Your Life on Purpose* (Berrett-Koehler Publishers, 2004), 125.

On the Heroic Journey, tangible symbols can be powerful markers, like road signs or cairns, telling us how far we must go and how far we have come. Think of ways you can symbolize this Journey to reinforce the significance of your Journey—in a drawing, a letter, a carving on a stick. Is there something you want to carry on your Journey to leave as a gift? I have friends who have walked the Camino de Santiago in Spain and left various items upon their completion. Even walking a labyrinth can symbolize an emotional journey. Is there an attitude or a behavior or a remembrance that you want to forget? Is there something you want to pick up on your Journey that you want to carry back into your life? The more we symbolize our life experiences, the more we connect to them and the more we are attuned to their gifts. What will you do to mark the significance of your purpose?

2. My car license plate says "CREATE" and I display it proudly, proclaiming what I want to do in the world every day. Tanya's license plate reads "BLISFUL." Identify what *your* word would be on a license plate and put it out in the world!
3. After my first divorce, I was so devastated at the loss of what I thought was supposed to be a forever marriage. While I am generally not a tattoo guy, I decided to ritualize this experience by getting a black tattoo of a wild horse in a Japanese brush painting style as a symbol of never losing my power and letting myself be "reined in" again. This symbol is very important for me to gather my strength, resolve, and power and step more confidently into an unknown future.

Take time to do something like this for yourself.

For Use in a Wilderness Setting

1. On an Outward Bound–type trip with friends, draw your purpose as a symbol on a piece of canvas. Clip it to a carabiner and then pass it around so everyone is aware of each other's purpose as you "carry" the intention of your purpose through the day.
2. Walk out in a natural setting and pick up something that represents your purpose today.
3. Plan a hike to a summit—small or large. Draw on a piece of paper what your purpose for that hike (or struggle) is. Carry it with you, and pull it out as a reminder when you are at the top.
4. Take a strip of colored cotton and write on it with a Sharpie your purpose for the day. Tie it on a branch of a tree in the wind like a prayer flag for your purpose.

NOTES

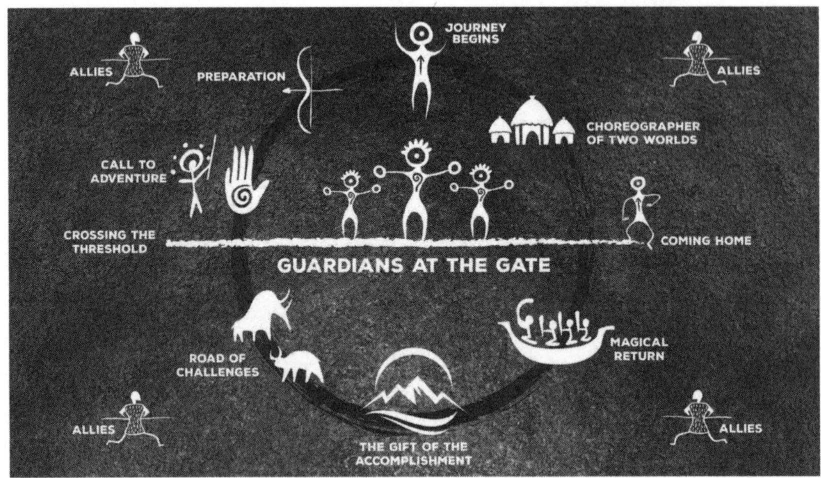

Chapter Nineteen

"A human being should be able to change a diaper, plan an invasion, butcher a hog, conn a ship, design a building, write a sonnet, balance accounts, build a wall, set a bone, comfort the dying, take orders, give orders, cooperate, act alone, solve equations, analyze a new problem, pitch manure, program a computer, cook a tasty meal, fight efficiently, die gallantly. Specialization is for insects."

—ROBERT A. HEINLEIN

The Preparation

Summary

The Preparation stage is an opportunity for us to take stock of our strengths and weaknesses—physically, mentally, emotionally, and spiritually. Like packing for an overseas trip or moving to Indonesia, this stage is where we lay everything out and see what we have. We get to decide what to take with us and what we might be lacking. Granted, we don't know what we will encounter, but taking stock is an important exercise, and it gets us thinking about what we might need and how we might get prepared.

The Preparation stage helps enhance our resiliency for the Journey ahead. The more resilient we are—developing what I call in my TEDx Talk "loose knees"—the more likely we will feel the adventurous spirit for what the Heroic Journey can offer. We can build resilience by developing ourselves so we are better able to face whatever the future, the "new normal," will bring. Ideally, if we are more aware of the various stages of the Heroic Journey, and practice the application and reflection exercises, we will have the benefit of a new perspective, which, in itself, can better prepare us for the ups and downs of life. This will make reentry and integration back from any experience less tumultuous and more fun and fulfilling.

A Word About Allies

While there will undoubtedly be Allies at every step of your Heroic Journey, they are called out at particular points around the circle model: Preparation, Road of Challenges, Magical Return, and Choreographer of Two Worlds.

The Allies can be real people, like family, friends, fellow military service or recovery members, or fellow climbers, or they can be "symbolic" Allies, like seeing an eagle soaring above you as you drive home from work. What is most important is that we start looking for and recognizing Allies who are a critical part of our Heroic Journey, even in the most unlikely places.

Questions

- In what ways have you taken stock and been prepared (or unprepared) in your life for Journeys you have made?

- Did you have a sense of excitement or fear?
- Who have been your Allies during times of Preparation? How have they helped you?
- The Heroic Journey Mindset suggests that we can think of the Preparation stage as what we will need for the Journey. What do these words mean to you? What other words work for you? How can these words help you tap into your Preparation stage for an upcoming Heroic Journey?
- What can you do to make this Preparation even better than your last?
- How can you better prepare mentally, physically, emotionally, and spiritually for the Journey into the unknown ahead?

Activities

1. Think about what you would want to pack if you were getting ready to run a marathon, going into a combat zone, going skiing, embarking on a recovery journey from addiction, moving to another country, changing jobs, or simply going to comfort a friend who is dying. Each of those events requires different physical, mental, emotional, and spiritual equipment. Make a list of things to prepare for an upcoming Heroic Journey.

Taking Stock: Present and Missing

William Stockton and Marjorie Herdes have been mentors and friends of mine for over three decades. They introduced me to the concept of seeing not what was wrong or broken, but looking for what was "present and missing." I have adapted their language here as a tool to do the same with our Taking Stock Activity.

Activity: Preparation—Taking Stock: Present and Missing

- Consider what you can do to better prepare for the unknown challenges that may lie ahead.
- Consider what you can do to bolster your resiliency on physical, mental, emotional, and spiritual levels.

Write your answers in the chart below.

TAKING STOCK	WHAT IS PRESENT?	WHAT IS MISSING?	HOW WILL I MAKE WHAT IS MISSING PRESENT?
Physically			
Mentally			
Emotionally			
Spiritually			
Allies	Who do I know who would help me?	Who should I know to help me?	How can I best access them?

2. Phil Hansen is a friend and a brilliant, gifted artist. Watch his TED Talk, "Embrace the Shake." How can you reframe

your choices and see the limitations ahead of you as your opportunity?

3. While it is important to think and have feelings about our Preparation, it can be helpful to share those thoughts and feelings with others or your Allies. Choose an Ally to speak with about an upcoming adventure or challenge.

NOTES

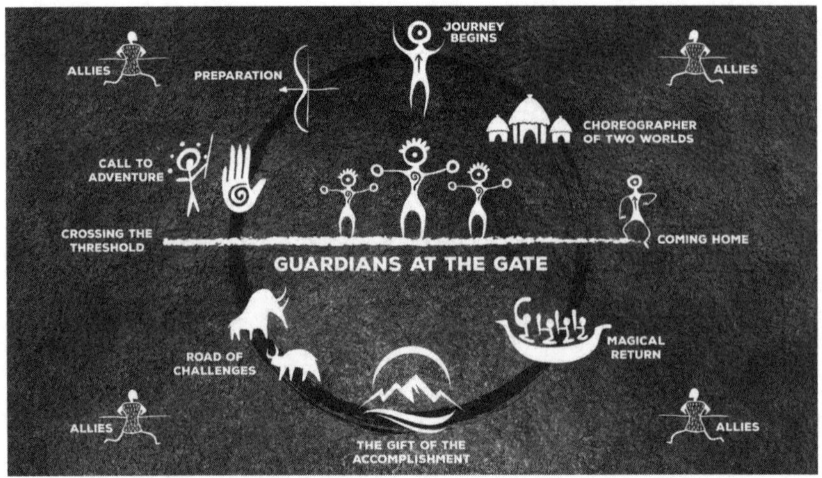

Chapter Twenty

"There are no mistakes. The events we bring upon ourselves, no matter how unpleasant, are necessary in order to learn what we need to learn; whatever steps we take, they're necessary to reach the places we've chosen to go. You are never given a wish without also being given the power to make it come true."

—RICHARD BACH

Our lives are an unending series of choices, options, precipitating events, and forks in many roads. I believe our Journey is about getting better at the discernment process for how we determine which choices, which options, and which forks to take. In my recovery process, I began to recognize the symbolic "rumble strips"—like those on a highway—that would caution me when I was veering from my intended path and in danger of going off the road. Wisdom encourages us to get good at identifying which Calls to Adventure will serve us and which ones will not.

The Call to Adventure

Summary

The Call to Adventure happens whenever there is an invitation to go somewhere or be a part of something new, or a circumstance happens that thrusts a person into a changed state. As we get more aware of ourselves in the Heroic Journey process, we become more conscious of the various forms of Calls to Adventure.

There is also the possibility of a "precipitating event," those changes that happen to us. These are the ones we cannot easily refuse—something that happens or a change in circumstances, such as a loved one getting sick or losing a limb or eyesight due to an accident. In these cases, the Call to Adventure challenges people to go where they might not otherwise choose to go.

As we mature in our understanding of the Heroic Journey, we get better at discerning with care the "call" to the next adventure. Rather than following along recklessly, we get to decide whether we even *want* to respond to the call. Some calls, it is important to note, are worth refusing. And if we say yes to the call, how might we apply what we have learned from previous experiences? For some of us, acceptance into a graduate program or a health challenge can be a "new call." We need to determine how the call fits into our lives and whether the new adventure is compelling or not. This is the point of either acceptance or refusal. If we are diagnosed with a life-threatening disease, we get to "choose" how we face that challenge, even though we might not be able to choose having it or not.

When my wife, Tanya, received her cancer diagnosis, she did not have a choice as to whether cancer was present in her body, but she did have a choice about how to face that fact. Erik Weihenmayer did not let the degenerative eye disorder that eventually took his sight stop him from summiting Mt. Everest. He did not choose retinoschisis, but he chose what to do in response.

The Call to Adventure in the Heroic Journey Mindset can be a turning point where we get in touch with our own spirit of adventure and begin to see our life choices as "adventures," not just uncomfortable challenges or pitfalls.

Questions

- What Calls to Adventure do you remember? Did you have a sense of an adventurous spirit? What made you decide to go?
- When have you "refused the call?" How do you feel about that decision now?
- Think about an upcoming Heroic Journey. What can you do to make this "adventure" even better than your last?
- The Heroic Journey Mindset suggests that we can think of Calls to Adventure as opportunities to experience something new and different. Can you use words like Power and Purpose as Tanya did to help you tap into your Call to Adventure for your upcoming Heroic Journey? What do these words mean to you? What other words work for you? My family had a saying when we were not sure whether to do something: "Well, we know what *not* doing it looks like." It often pushed us into saying yes to the new experience. How might considering *not* doing something you've been presented with change your mind? Is there something

you've been avoiding because it seems hard, which could, in the end, be better than saying no?

- Is your next Call to Adventure truly serving your highest good? If so, why? If not, why not?
- Think of a precipitating event that has occurred in your life—one that you need to respond to one way or another. How might you find a way for this precipitating event to best serve your life, family, or community?

Activities

1. Sir Ernest Shackleton, the great Antarctic explorer, was purported to have posted this advertisement in the Times of London in the 1900s, looking for people to join a dangerous expedition to Antarctica. Would you be compelled to join based on the words Shackleton picked? What would be compelling to you now? Why have you responded to your Call to Adventure?

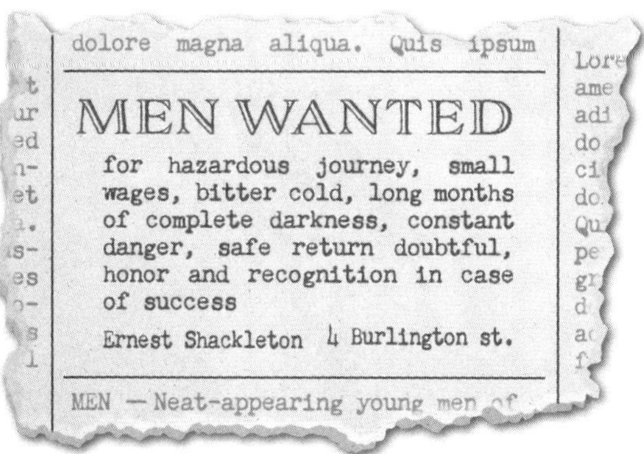
dolore magna aliqua. Quis ipsum

MEN WANTED

for hazardous journey, small wages, bitter cold, long months of complete darkness, constant danger, safe return doubtful, honor and recognition in case of success

Ernest Shackleton 4 Burlington st.

MEN — Neat-appearing young men of

2. Take a few minutes and craft an advertisement for the Call to Adventure you are about to go on . . .

- » Marriage
- » Overseas assignment
- » Personal health crisis
- » New job promotion or entrepreneurial launch
- » Day trip, hike, or glacier climb you are about to go on

3. How did you capture the Call to Adventure in your expedition advertisement? Did it change how you felt about it? Did it ignite your spirit of adventure?
4. Watch the inspirational YouTube video about Richie Parker at Hendrik Motors:

5. How did Richie Parker take on each Call to Adventure? How did he seem to embody them?
6. Watch the inspirational video of triathlete Sarah Reinertsen:

How did Sarah Reinertsen take on each Call to Adventure? How did she seem to embody the adventurous spirit in her Call to Adventure?

NOTES

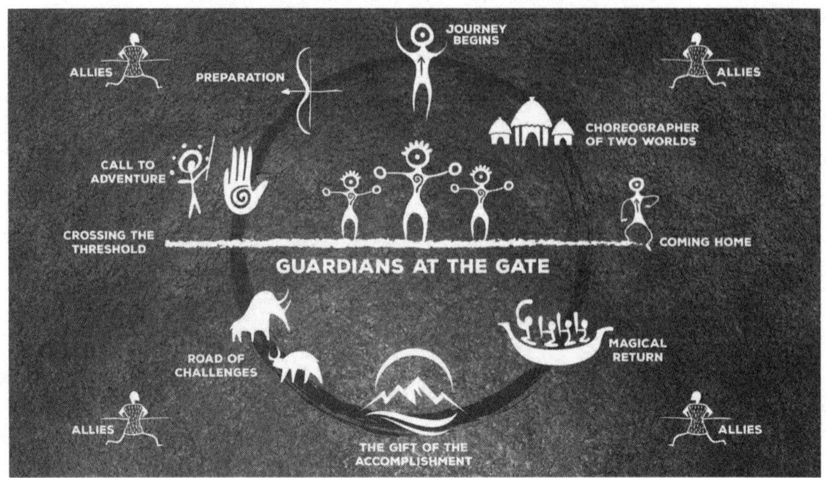

Chapter Twenty-One

"You must never be fearful about what you are doing when it's right."

—ROSA PARKS

Once we have identified the Calls to Adventure and discerned our need to continue forward, then we are ready to move on to the next stage. We are ready to jump across a symbolic, or sometimes very real, boundary. We are ready to step into our new choice. Get ready, things are going to get interesting!

Crossing the Threshold—Guardians at the Gate

Summary

Crossing the Threshold is about taking steps to move forward in response to the Call to Adventure. This is the point when the Guardians at the Gate appear, whose job it is to challenge our intentions and our convictions for the choices we have made. These symbolic Guardians often seem adversarial, as they jab pointed questions at us, such as

- Who do you think *you* are?
- Where do you think *you're* going?
- Why have you come?
- What good do you think you will do?

Crossing the Threshold can be the act of applying to a graduate program, showing up for training, or getting on a plane to a distant location. This is when reality has set in. Crossing the Threshold is also a symbolic move from a position of certainty to one of uncertainty, of not knowing what lies ahead and having real doubts as to whether we are up to the challenge. The Guardians at the Gate can appear in many forms—real people who present resistance or as physical roadblocks such as flat tires, ruined or unreadable maps, bad weather, etc.

Each of us needs to wrestle with the questions the Guardians at the Gate pose and find ways to handle the resistance that comes from people who may appear to be roadblocks on our Journey. Steven Pressfield, in his profoundly useful book *The War of Art*, speaks of "resistance" as the Guardians at the Gate that will try and thwart every important thing you do.[5] I highly recommend his book to help you learn to overcome the "resistance" you will face in its many forms. Knowing what I know now has improved my ability to handle the Guardians at the Gate every time I face them. These insights about "learning from our roadblocks" can be key learning opportunities as our Journeys continue.

Questions

- How have you Crossed the Thresholds before in your life?
- What has been your experience with Guardians at the Gate?
- As you Cross the Threshold into this new experience, what barriers (human or situational) are presenting themselves and what can you learn from them?
- How can you change your response so that you are looking into the future and moving forward with stronger, more powerful self-encouraging language that gives you a "stronger arm" than before?
- How can setting positive, strong intentions play a key part in developing your Heroic Journey Mindset?

Activities

1. **Strong Thoughts—Strong Arm:** One of the best ways to practice Crossing the Threshold is to practice an aikido

---

5 Steven Pressfield, *The War of Art: Break Through the Blocks and Win Your Inner Creative Battles* (Black Irish Entertainment LLC, 2012).

training technique I learned from friend and colleague Brian Green, which is easy to do and portable.

» Ask a friend or family member to demonstrate this with you by holding their arm out straight from their shoulder with an open hand, palm facing up. Ask them to think about a worry in their head: something that makes them sad, mad, or frustrated. As they do, gently pull down on their arm to feel the resistance. Usually, you are able to pull it down quite easily.

» Now, ask the same person to clear their mind and take a couple of easy, deep breaths. This time, ask them to point their arm toward the horizon, open palm. Have them think of their own strength, of their capacity to overcome challenges, and to have those thoughts flow down their arm through their fingertips and out to the farthest horizon they can see. As they do, gently pull down on their arm to feel the resistance. Usually, it is recognizably different. Their arm feels like a full extension of their intentions and is harder to pull down.

» After your friend has done it, switch around for you to try it. Practice both the "worried weak arm" and the "intentional stronger arm" techniques so they can see the difference for themselves.

» How did the Strong Thoughts—Strong Arm activity go for you? Did you notice any difference in your partner's strength from the first time to the second time? Did you notice any difference in your own two times? What were the differences and how did you interpret that?

This activity helps us see the power of intention when we Cross the Threshold. As we approach the Threshold and are confronted by the Guardians, whatever they may be, we have a couple of choices—wither with worry or get strong with intention. Both approaches can have a significant impact on our ability to achieve what we have set out to accomplish.

The Strong Thoughts—Strong Arm activity can be a great reminder of how important the voices in our heads can be. We can use them at any point and teach this activity to others when you observe people having difficulty.

When Brian Green and I facilitate ropes courses with corporate leadership groups, we always start with this activity, to help people identify how much stronger they are when they speak to themselves with positive messages versus negative messages. It really works!

While it is important to think about and feel what Crossing the Threshold and our Guardians at the Gate might be, it can be really helpful to discuss with others and your Allies. Choose an Ally to talk with about this concept.

NOTES

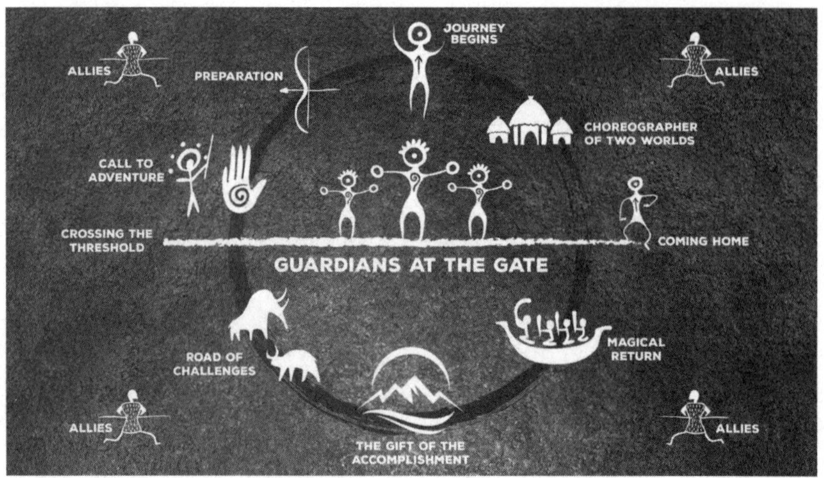

Chapter Twenty-Two

"There is a tremendous strength that is growing in the world through sharing together, praying together, suffering together, and working together."

—MOTHER TERESA

We have heard the Call to Adventure, we have discerned that we have what it takes to answer the call by Crossing the Threshold and dodging the Guardians at the Gate, and we stand in our new choice, our new world. And it sometimes doesn't feel very good. I remember a mentor telling me once, "When we do the right thing for the first time, it feels wrong." Again, we summon the courage to begin the hard stage known as the Road of Challenges.

Road of Challenges

Summary

The next stage is where we meet our new teachers, often struggle with our hardest assignments, and face tests that can be viewed either as opportunities or setbacks. Whether it's a cancer diagnosis, loss of a job, a challenging pregnancy, or marital problems, the Road of Challenges is where each person faces their most difficult trials—mentally, physically, emotionally, and spiritually. Without preparing well for this and not having developed and engaged solid and dependable Allies, a person can be in for a truly difficult time. While some people seem to weather the storm with grace and dignity, others, sadly, struggle through their Road of Challenges. Learning you have the ability to control your attitude during times of adversity and hardship is part of this Journey. I have heard military vets refer to this stage as a time to "suffer well." By "suffering well," we are developing our loose knees as part of our Heroic Journey Mindset.

Each of us has experienced numerous difficulties on our own Road of Challenges, from things that happened to us as kids to things that happened to us in the service or on missions . . . and even when we got back home. The key thing is that each of us has survived up to this point. We dug down deep inside ourselves and found something that got us through those painful experiences, those "dark nights of the soul." We learned how to survive all the things that could have broken our spirit or killed us. We learned that since we survived that difficult time, we can "suffer well" and get through other things that may be ahead. The Heroic Journey Mindset reminds us to keep the positive intention from our last Strong Thoughts—Strong Arm activity and bring it to the Road of Challenges so that we have positive energy as we take on new challenges. Like Tanya, pick your strong support words, like Power and Purpose. Remember, attitude is everything!

Questions

- What have been some of your previous Roads of Challenges? How have you handled them on different Journeys of your life?
- How well are you handling a Road of Challenges you are experiencing now?
- What can you do to improve your attitude to better handle the challenges you are facing?
- What can you do to embrace the spirit of Viktor Frankl, who said, "To choose one's attitude in any given set of circumstances is to choose one's own way,"[6] so you can improve your attitude on the Road of Challenges?
- How can this help you reframe major setbacks to see them as smaller inconveniences? It is easy to gripe and swear when we get a flat tire when we are driving. But it takes courage and a sense of humor to say, "Kids, have you ever changed a flat tire before? Here we go!"

Questions About the Role of Allies

- What has been your experience with Allies during your Road of Challenges?
- How did they show up for you?
- Were you surprised by their support?
- Were they real people . . . or were they symbolic?
- How can you be sure to avail yourself of the powerful connection with Allies this time?

---

6 Frankl, *Man's Search for Meaning*.

Activities

Erik Weihenmayer and his Mt. Everest ascent team members had a fun technique they used to keep their attitude positive, in even the most difficult times. He called it "Positive Pessimism." When he was clinging to a freezing cliff edge on Mt. Everest, at 28,000 feet, he would yell down to his climbing partners, "Sure is cold . . . but at least it's windy!" or "Whew, this pack is really heavy, but at least it's lopsided."

When I was running a wilderness program with South Bronx high school students and we got caught in a torrential downpour, I asked them to playfully repeat the phrase I had taught them as we huddled under dripping tarps. They all responded with humor: "This is just the way we like it!"

My friend Mary Beth Lamb, when she was going through her own cancer chemo treatments, brought her own version of positivity in challenging times. She would put on boxing gloves and an oversized silk boxing robe and dance around the other women at the chemo center encouraging the others, "C'mon girls, we are fighting today!"

1. See if you can come up with "Positive Pessimism" phrases to get you through a hard challenge with a smile on your face. Helping others find humor in difficult circumstances is a noble task and gets us out of ourselves as well. Share them with others who are also on a similar Journey as you think of them.
2. While it is important to think and feel what our Roads of Challenges have been, it can be really helpful to share those thoughts, feelings, and stories with others and your Allies. Choose an Ally to talk with about this concept.

NOTES

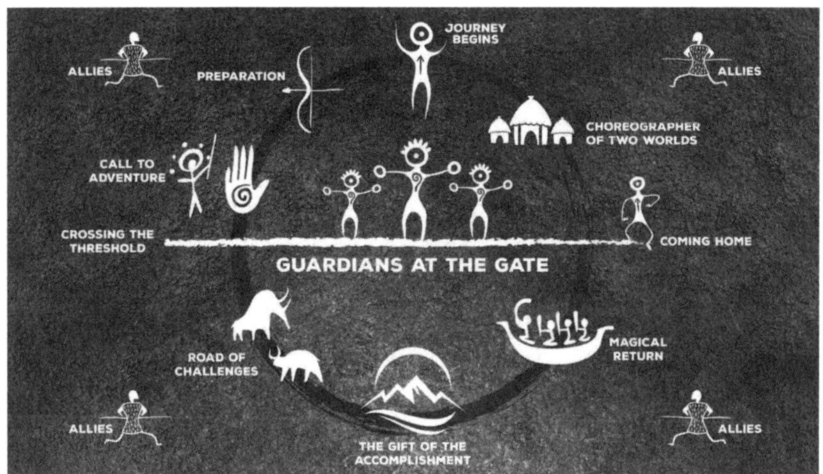

Chapter Twenty-Three

"None of us chose the circumstances of our birth. We had nothing to do with having been born into privilege or under stigma. We have everything to do with what we do with our God-given talents and how we treat others in our species from this day forward."

—ISABEL WILKERSON

After the darkness of the cold winter night, after the rain lets up from the monsoon, there is a sunrise, a symbolic awakening on the other side of our Road of Challenges. We have reached our proverbial summit, and we stand looking down on all Creation.

The Gift of the Accomplishment

Summary

Those who survive their Road of Challenges need to determine the Gift embedded in the experience. This is often a deeply internal and sometimes difficult search—to discover the Gifts inherent in hardship and adversity.

It is my experience that when our skills have matched the levels of a hard challenge and we have climbed the proverbial mountain and stood on the summit, we are often flooded with purpose, gratitude, and even joy. Something magical has happened to us. We have come through the dark night of the soul and turned the bow of the previously outward-bound ship toward home. It is critical at this point in the process to understand what the Gift is. We must name it and protect it in order to carry it forward into our next endeavor.

This is a good time to reconnect to the original purpose of your Heroic Journey that you focused on in the first stage. Sometimes during our struggle to accomplish something difficult, different purposes are revealed to us—different from the one we may have chosen when we started our Heroic Journey.

The founders and authors of *The Big Book of Alcoholics Anonymous*, no strangers to hardship, have written about the power of resilience and acceptance in helping people see the Gift in their discovery of their alcoholism and the Accomplishment of daily victories over addiction.

Here are two short readings that address acceptance as a gift:

"God grant me the serenity to accept the things I cannot change, courage to change the things I can, and the wisdom to know the difference." [known as The Serenity Prayer]

"And acceptance is the answer to all my problems today. When I am disturbed, it is because I find some person, place, thing, or situation—some fact of my life—unacceptable to me, and I can find no serenity until I accept that person, place, thing, or situation as being exactly the way it is supposed to be at this moment. Nothing, absolutely nothing, happens in God's world by mistake. Until I could accept my alcoholism, I could not stay sober; unless I accept life completely on life's terms, I cannot be happy. I need to concentrate not so much on what needs to be changed in the world as on what needs to be changed in me and in my attitudes."[7]

Questions

- How have you identified Gifts, Accomplishments, and Purpose in your life from the Heroic Journeys you have made?
- What was the Gift or Gifts given to you from this experience?
- How can you take this Gift with you moving forward?
- How can you practice seeing the Gifts in the terrible things that may have happened to you?

Activities

1. **Leave Something, Take Something:** Think back to your first stage of the Heroic Journey, when we asked you to define your purpose. As a reminder:

   Think of ways you can symbolize this Journey to reinforce the significance of your Journey—in a drawing, a letter, a carving on a stick. Is there something you want to carry on your Journey to leave as a gift? Is there an attitude or behavior or a remembrance that you want to forget? Is there something you want to pick up on your Journey

7 Bill Wilson, *Big Book of Alcoholics Anonymous*, 4th ed. (Alcoholics Anonymous World Service, 2001), 417.

that you want to carry back into your life? The more we symbolize our life experiences, the more we connect to them, and the more we are attuned to their Gifts. What will you do to mark the significance of your purpose?

What was it you did to symbolize your Heroic Journey? Take out the stone, stick, or letter that you wrote and spend some time with it, reliving the pictures in your mind from points along the Heroic Journey that got you to your "summit." How does it seem now, at the midpoint of your Heroic Journey? Is your purpose still the same or has it changed? If so, how? Ask yourself, *How have I changed?* What have you liked, or not liked, about the changes?

Now it is time for the second half of the activity.

- Stop doing: How can you symbolize what you want to stop doing going forward?
- Start doing: How can you symbolize what you want to start doing going forward?
- Keep doing: How can you symbolize what you want to keep doing going forward?

Personally, I love symbolizing experience. Whenever something big happens, I memorialize it in a stone, a found object, or a memento that I can carry with me. I can be in a corporate office setting and reach into my pocket and feel a stone from the island of Iona in Scotland or a recovery coin, and I am grounded in the Gifts of those experiences.

2. While it is important to think and feel what our purpose might have been and our experiences with the Gift and the Accomplishment, it can be really helpful if you share those thoughts and feelings with others or your Allies. Choose an Ally to talk with about this concept.

NOTES

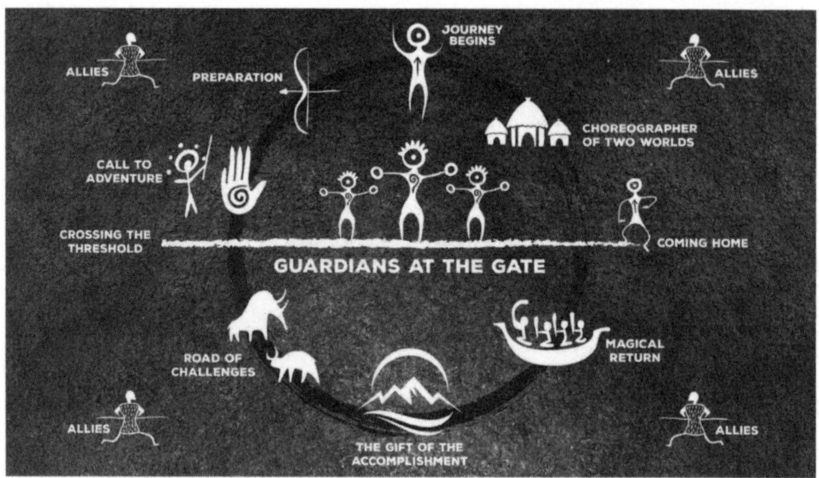

Chapter Twenty-Four

"If you own this story you get to write the ending."

—BRENÉ BROWN

We have reached the summit of our Heroic Journey, we have survived the sublime or the unspeakable, and we are turning back for home. We are exhausted. We are ecstatic. And we need to be really careful. We have to negotiate our Return and bring back what we have learned as if it were a dozen precious raw eggs.

The Magical Return

Summary

Upon return from the summit of a mountain, many people are elated with their accomplishments and yet are potentially at risk due to fatigue or an injury from the dangers of the down climb. We can benefit greatly from more intentional processing time in the Return stage. Too often, our fast-paced culture denies time to process or assemble learnings from one experience to another.

This stage is called the Magical Return because it is when you have just accomplished something really big or endured or "suffered well" through something that was the hardest thing you have ever faced. At these points in our lives, we naturally are rather self-focused; after all, look what we just did!

However, the Heroic Journey Mindset has a way of bringing us back to a different focus, one which includes more awareness of the well-being of those around us in addition to ourselves. One of my favorite quotes by C. S. Lewis is about humility: "Humility is not thinking less of ourselves, it is thinking of ourselves less often."[8]

It is an important reminder that we very likely could not have accomplished what we just accomplished or suffered through what we endured without other people's help. It is one of many times we need to think about other people and how we might help them return from big experiences as well.

The Magical Return is where Allies can help us, and we can help others as Allies. We think we are going to have an easy, fun Return from our big experiences, but often that is not the case. This is where we begin the Return to our previous lives, and even though we think we have accomplished the big thing, like climbing Devils Tower

---

8 C. S. Lewis, *Mere Christianity* (Harper San Francisco, 2001).

in Wyoming, we still have to get down safely. We need to gather a bit more seriousness about us and start to prepare for the Return Journey. When I lead multiple-day corporate leadership retreats, I caution the participants that this is a crucial and often overlooked stage and that we need to start "packing for the return trip."

Questions

- How have you identified the Magical Return in your life for Journeys you have made?
- In what ways can you take the best of the Gifts and Accomplishments you have gained and internalize them, so you can carry them forward with intention and integrity?
- What **Stop Doing, Start Doing, Keep Doing** activity from the last section can you commit to, and how can you help hold yourself and others accountable for accomplishing new goals?
- How does the Magical Return fit into your purpose for this Heroic Journey, for reentry to your life?

Questions About the Role of Allies

- How have you noticed Allies in the Magical Return stage of the Heroic Journey?
- How have they helped you in your Return?
- Were they real people or symbolic Allies?

Activities

1. **Appreciation Circle:** Each person on a Heroic Journey has been helped by some other person somewhere along the way. An Appreciation Circle is when we circle back and thank them for the part they played in our Journey. When Tanya completed her cancer treatments, she told each of the doctors and nurses how important they had been in her recovery. This seems simple, and yet, it does two things: It thanks people for the role they played in our Heroic Journeys and also begins to get us out of our heads for the Magical Return by helping us realize it is not only about us.

Examples:

- "I want to appreciate Bill and Carol because they worked with me in Arizona when I was going through a really dark period of my life."
- "I want to appreciate John because he stuck with me all those years of my early sobriety as my sponsor."

Think of someone you'd like to appreciate and journal about it. If you feel comfortable, ideally, tell that person what impact they made on your Journey. How did you feel during the Appreciation Circle? What came up for you?

Appreciation Circles can be a powerful experience for some people, both in taking time to recognize someone else and also being on the receiving end of the experience, where someone honors you for a selfless act.

2. While it is important to think and feel what our Magic Return might have been, it can be really helpful to share those thoughts and feelings with others or with Allies. Choose an Ally to talk with about this concept.

NOTES

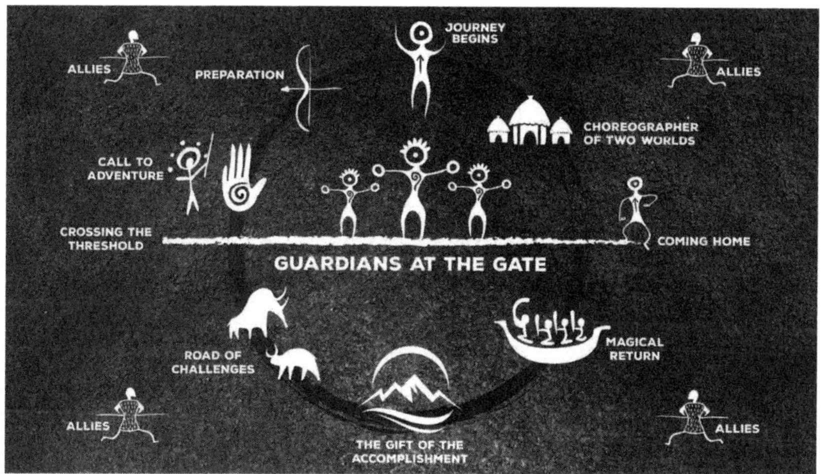

Chapter Twenty-Five

"You gain strength, courage, and confidence by every experience in which you really stop to look fear in the face. You are able to say to yourself, 'I lived through this horror. I can take the next thing that comes along.'"

—ELEANOR ROOSEVELT

We not only have to return to our homes of origin, we are now carrying the dozen precious raw eggs of our new, tender selves and all that we have learned. And, to make matters even more challenging, we need to dodge those pesky Guardians of the Gate again. If you can picture the brilliant actor Jackie Chan protecting a dozen eggs as he fights off a hoard of oncoming ninjas, the image might be close to what this is going to take for us to get past them this time.

Coming Home—Guardians at the Gate Again

Summary

Upon returning from the adventure, our self-focused elation meets the Guardians at the Gate, who once again question our intentions and convictions. We have met the Guardians at the Gate on the way out to our adventure when the Journey began, and even though these Guardians might be different, we should be better prepared to dart past them as we Return. We know now that they try to push us back as a way to teach us lessons.

Preparation for Coming Home is as, if not more, important as the Preparation at the beginning of a Journey. For example, when returning from an overseas assignment, it's essential for military veterans to remember they have had an incredibly challenging experience—and one many others have not had in the same way. They have been caught up in the sights, sounds, and smells of another country. Yet others might dismiss it as a "free vacation" from the day-to-day grind of life and simply minimize the experience because they don't comprehend all that may have happened to them internally.

When we reenter from a big experience, we are often "shut down" or minimized by Guardians who don't seem to appreciate what we have been through. We have just had the most incredible experience and we are headed home . . . only to be stopped in our tracks, sometimes physically, by border guards, bureaucratic red tape, and people who don't appreciate what we have done. We are in danger of losing the really good feeling and the Gifts of our Accomplishments by wrestling with the Guardians on their terms.

We must tap back into ourselves and revisit our purpose that we initially had when we set out to do the Heroic Journey, as well as the purpose we may have discovered along the way and the Gifts we have received from this particular Heroic Journey. All of this will help us reclaim who we are and how we have changed, so we can keep the benefits of the Journey and not slip back into the person they want us to be back home.

Often, we suffer in silence, because we don't have people to talk to about this, or we don't think people will understand. Here is another checkpoint to develop our relationship with our Allies—people who know us and know our Journey. They have been here, or a place very similar to here before. They can help us.

Remember the questions they asked us before? They will try and push back and ask you again:

- Who do you think *you* are?
- Where do you think *you're* going?
- Why have you come?
- What good do you think you will do?

This time, be ready by deeply owning your experiences and learning. If you are solid in your core beliefs, they will not topple you over. It is only when we are stuck in our head, focusing on ourselves and our little accomplishments coming back from our Magical Return, that we are weak. Own your experience. Recognize the Allies and people who have helped you, and tell them you appreciate what they did. If we do this, we will beat these buggers.

Questions

- Think about a past Return that did not feel so "heroic." What could you have done differently to reenter your "normal" life with more ease and less stress?
- What will you take away from that Coming Home experience and use to apply to your life coming back this time?

- Think about a Heroic Journey you are presently on. How can you best prepare for Coming Home by bolstering your resilience and your "loose knees" on the physical, mental, emotional, and spiritual levels?
- What did you learn about the Guardians at the Gate the first time you met them that might help you to dodge past them or minimize their power over you on your way back home?
- How can you reclaim the Gifts you have gained from your Journey so that you feel stronger?

Activities

1. Remember when we first met the Guardians at the Gate and we did the Strong Thoughts—Strong Arm activity? How has that helped you? Were you able to call upon the power of Strong Thoughts?

One of the best ways to practice Coming Home and meeting the Guardians at the Gate again is to practice the same aikido training technique. We can do this activity again and again as a reminder of how Strong Thoughts help us in the face of adversity, even when facing the Guardians at the Gate. I like to paraphrase what Steven Pressfield says in *The War of Art*: We need to become professionals at fighting the resistance to us coming back better people. We need to turn pro.[9]

2. While it is important to think and feel what our Coming Home and what our meeting the Guardians at the Gate again might be like, it can be really helpful to share those thoughts and feelings with others and your Allies. Choose an Ally to talk with about this concept.

9 Pressfield, *The War of Art*, 62–96.

NOTES

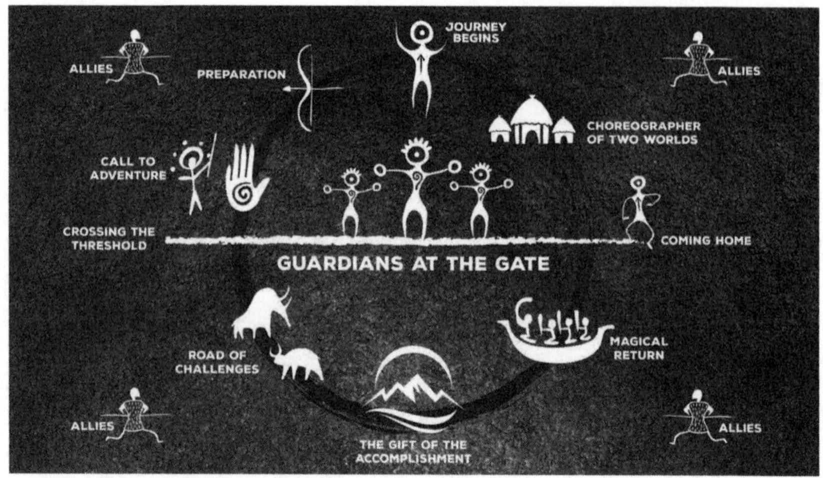

Chapter Twenty-Six

"You are always free to change your mind and choose a different future, or a different past."

—RICHARD BACH

And now that we are returning from all that has transpired on our Heroic Journey, we are not the same person we once were. We are different. Like a hermit crab that outgrew its shell and set off to find a new one, we are no longer able to fit into the old shell if we were to try it on for size. Which means we now know Two Worlds: the one we left and the one we are returning to now. We are that different.

The Choreographer of Two Worlds

Summary

A perspective that is critical for reentry is that of a Choreographer of Two Worlds. Those on the Journey know what they have just been through, but it is difficult for people back home to understand. So, in a sense, we are now living in two worlds. While it is critical to take time to evaluate our own Journey, we also need to be sensitive to what the Journey has been for people who were back home or back in the office.

When we Come Home, not only have we accomplished big things, but we sometimes forget that we have lost things, and that our family and friends have also lost things in the Journey. Reentry is particularly difficult when the realization of these losses hits us unexpectedly. It was almost a relief when I realized that the Choreographer of Two Worlds simply means that I have two worlds spinning in my head, one from my Heroic Journey and one of my back-home world. The challenge now becomes one of integration. Integration begins with awareness of what we have lost or won from our Journey, our acceptance of that fact, and what we can do about it moving forward.

If we do a short assessment and begin to name the "losses" as well as the "wins," we will have an easier time adapting to the two worlds: our Journey world and our back-home world.

Questions

- How have you identified being a Choreographer of Two Worlds on other Journeys you have made?

Activities

Assessment of Wins: I did my master's thesis on both the Heroic Journey and William Bridges's change management model. He suggests that to go through change, we need to be keenly aware of what losses are actually happening to us as well as others. This chart is inspired by the work he created in his book *Managing Transitions*. Think of a Heroic Journey you have been on in the past or are currently on and fill out the following charts.

- Which of these losses are you experiencing?
- Which of these losses are your family and friends experiencing?

SELF	YOUR FAMILY/ FRIENDS	LOSS OF:
☐	☐	**Relationship(s)** • Loss of membership, reporting relationships (employee-employer), groups, and friends
☐	☐	**Identity** • Loss of the familiar: Responsibilities, recognition for work that is no longer necessary, title, and group name
☐	☐	**Skills** • Loss of physical strength or capability/way of doing things, comfortable routines or procedures
☐	☐	**Future** • Loss of unrealized dreams or potential, what we thought would happen and doesn't
☐	☐	**Meaning or Purpose** • Not understanding why things had to happen, not seeing how they connect or fit into the "big picture," and not seeing the purpose or feeling fulfillment
☐	☐	**Influence** • A feeling of importance has been replaced by a feeling of powerlessness to affect the outcomes. You might say, "People used to ask me for my opinions before, but now it seems that no one is interested."
☐	☐	**Control** • Loss of ability to make own decisions and be more in control of situations
☐	☐	**Tradition** • Loss of tradition may include changing values, beliefs, practices, history, and culture
☐	☐	**Others?**

- Which of these wins are you experiencing?
- Which of these wins are your family and friends experiencing?

SELF	YOUR FAMILY/ FRIENDS	GAIN OF:
☐	☐	**Relationship(s)** • Increased feelings of membership; reporting relationships, groups, and new friends; reconnection with family
☐	☐	**Identity** • Expansion of the familiar: new responsibilities, recognition for work that you have accomplished, title, and group name
☐	☐	**Skills** • Increase of physical capacity/way of working, expanded and comfortable routines or procedures
☐	☐	**Future** • Enhanced sense of realizing dreams or potential; setting a goal and despite challenges, achieving it
☐	☐	**Meaning or Purpose** • Deeper understanding of what your purpose and why are, gratefully seeing how they connect or fit into the "big picture," and feeling a sense of fulfillment
☐	☐	**Influence** • A growing feeling of importance, of being able to affect change and outcomes; recognition that you, as well as other people, value what you contribute
☐	☐	**Control** • Ability to make own decisions and be more in control of situations
☐	☐	**Tradition** • Feeling a strong and nurturing connection to tradition, values, beliefs, practices, history, and culture
☐	☐	**Others?**

By taking these short assessments as a pulse check, you can quickly see where you and others are benefiting from the Gifts and Accomplishments from your Heroic Journey or suffering from a difficult Return as a Choreographer of Two Worlds.

- How can you improve your ability to see both worlds and learn to speak "two languages" to better ease your reentry?
- How can you help other people and ease their pain as a way of helping you reenter as well?

1. While it is important to think and feel what our Choreographer of Two Worlds might be like, it can be really helpful if you share those thoughts and feelings with others and your Allies. Choose an Ally to talk with about this concept.

NOTES

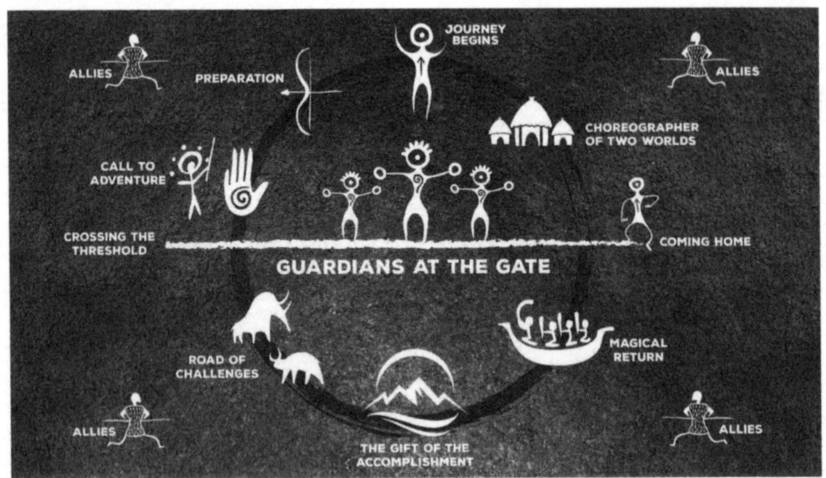

Chapter Twenty-Seven

"For there is always light. If only we're brave enough to see it.
If only we're brave enough to be it."

—AMANDA GORMAN

Every day, we have the opportunity to begin again. Before every Heroic Journey, we begin as a caterpillar, and after the Journey, emerge into the light much like a butterfly breaking through the cocoon into our new world. We allow ourselves a minute to pause, opening and closing our wings as they dry. We feel their new strength. We have within us a new sense of ourselves. We look around us at the world we once knew and see it with new eyes. Where once we crawled, now we fly.

Beginning Anew
Summary

Before we begin the next Heroic Journey, it is important that we integrate what we have learned from our last Journey.

The Return Home is a literal return to our place of origin, but we are not necessarily the same people we were when we started. To help us fully integrate back home, we need to be aware of what we lost, what we have gained, and how we have grown from the experience. We also need to celebrate the Return in very real and also symbolic ways. That is the first order of business: celebrate. We honor the fact that we made it home, that we accomplished something (big or small—however it looks to the outside world, we know it meant something important to us).

One thing to remember: We sought and found Allies along the way to help us, and we should appreciate them and include them in our celebration. And then, one of the greatest gifts of all can be when we realize that we can serve as an Ally for others. Once we have been on a challenging "adventure," and see it as a Heroic Journey, then we can be more readily available as Allies to help others on their Journeys.

Lastly, after the celebration comes Preparation for the future. This stage is about taking the time to stop and reflect on our previous Heroic Journey and all the stages along the way. Much like we did at the beginning of the Preparation stage, we need to "take stock" and see what we have at the end of our Journey . . . kind of like checking after a short trip whether we needed to bring all the stuff we did and make a mental note of bringing something we needed but didn't have.

Questions

- What have you done or will you do to celebrate a Heroic Journey you have completed?
- Examples from some people I know:
  a. Throwing a celebration party (large and small)
  b. Going on a trip into the wilderness for solo time
  c. Starting a fitness plan to stay in shape now that they are in shape
  d. Getting a particular tattoo to symbolize what they just went through
- What did I learn from my last Heroic Journey?
- What can I do to better prepare for the unknown challenges that may lie ahead?
- What can I do to bolster my resiliency on physical, mental, emotional, and spiritual levels? Write your answers in the following chart as you reflect on your last Heroic Journey.

Activities

1. Fill out the following chart, detailing what remained after a Heroic Journey you took and how that aids you in preparing for Journeys to come.

TAKING STOCK	WHAT IS PRESENT NOW?	WHAT IS MISSING NOW?	WHAT WILL I DO NEXT TIME TO GET WHAT IS MISSING PRESENT?
PHYSICALLY			
MENTALLY			
EMOTIONALLY			
SPIRITUALLY			

- What did you discover by spending a few minutes with the Present and Missing Chart from your Heroic Journey?
- Having completed this adventure, this Heroic Journey, how can you take what you have learned and be more intentional about your experience on your next Journey and more available to help others on their Journeys?

2. While it is important to think and feel what our Coming Home might have been, it can be really helpful to share those thoughts and feelings with others and your Allies. As always, choose an Ally to talk with about this concept.

NOTES

[Taken from the author's balcony.]

Afterword

"The quality of strength lined with tenderness is an unbeatable combination."

—MAYA ANGELOU

Here is my personal congratulations to each of you for taking on this work yourselves and reframing painful situations in your lives that you have carried long enough. I honor you for who you are and how you are choosing to be in the world. You are making a huge difference, every day. In sometimes small and seemingly simple ways, they each add up on a significant cosmic level to increase the balance of good in the world.

Thank you!

Your ally,

Peter Hitchcock Bailey

Sending you light and love—Blessings on your journey of reframing your life!

Acknowledgments

I am who I am because of many people. And I am grateful for each and every person I have met and have learned to appreciate. Many will not be mentioned, but a few particularly impactful people come to mind. I note them here with profound gratitude.

Eric Wright, Jan Wright, Professor Baylor Johnson, Professor John Barthelme, Professor Thomas Coburn, Patricia Neal, Craig Neal, Dr. Jasper Hunt, Dr. Bob Vanderwilt, Dr. Cohen, Jiff Quinn Blansfield, Dawes Walter, John Rathbun, Loren Hoyman, Ed Tittel, Bill Coleman, Carol Ross, Lisa Sprague, William Frost, Tim Vallilee, Ben Quie, Joe Sprague, John Littlefield, Sam Trudell, Marjorie Herdes, Will Stockton, Miss Petty, Kevin Stewart, Mary Beth Lamb, Richard Leider, Jim Kielsmeier, Mac Hall, Rocky Kimball, Cath Crooks, Dan Nietz, Paul Stoltz, Ronda Beaman, Margie Adler, Nate Garvis, Jennifer McLeod, Edwin Banks, Fred Bobich, Phil Hansen, Annis Parker, Dr. Henry Emmons, CathyAnn Beaty, Erik Weihenmayer, John O'Leary, Erica Leder, Mark Walinske, Kristin Stolte, Brian Green, Patrick Mosher, Cecily Sommers, Chris Everett, Ann Cahill, Jim Cahill, Jeff Dayton, Scott Schwefel, Andy Lothian, Jim Kirchman, Bill Winter, Hugh McCormack, Tom Joyce, Ben Zander, Steven Pressfield, Cynthia Wold, William Bridges, Took Osborn, Peter Himmelman, Lisa Brotzler, and John Schmidt, one of the kindest guys I know, and so many others!

A grateful hug to my fellow Fire Circle men for being such generous and wise witnesses of each other's lives: David O'Fallon,

David McNally, Dave Wagner, Tom Wiese, John Wright, Tony Peet, Don Damond, Dion Hughes, Tim Day, Vikas Narula, Jeff Sylvester, Michael Bischoff, Eric Elwer, Jack Frangipane, Corey Jensen, Chris Heim, Kirby Johnson, Jeff Steinke, Api Sulistyo, Carl Blanz.

Special shout out to my COLT brothers and sisters: Rick Nelson, Dave Comeau, Dan Margo, Chuck Campbell, Keith Baker, Ruth and Scott Harris, Beki Saito, and Deb Howard. We have been through a lot together and we have many more life adventures ahead!

Grateful thanks to the team at The Prouty Project for sharing in my learning journey and making work so fun: Jeff Prouty, Sam Smith, Adrienne Jordan, Mike Felmlee, Kristin Jonason, Bethany Krueger, Samantha Harris, Kari Baltzer, Julie Marks, Tammy Pearson, Paige Prouty, Jonah Kandikatla and Lexi Wick.

Special mention and appreciation to Michael Campbell at Radiate Presentation Design for his vision and work with the Heroic Journey graphic.

And to Marion Roach Smith, whose skills with words—her own and others'—was the driving force behind getting this book written.

Deep thanks to my editorial and publishing team at Greenleaf Book Group: Brian Welch, Trinity Massengale, Jenea Havener, Hayden Seder, Melinda Andrews, Jonathan Lewis, HaJ, Rachel High, Valerie Howard, Tanya Hall, and the entire team behind the scenes. Thank you for seeing the value of this book and helping to make it better so that it mattered!

And, of course, to my amazing, loving, inspiring family who have taught me so much: Tanya, Sydney and Jackson, Pamela Bailey, Tom Joyce, Siglinde Moore, the entire Hitchcock and Bailey extended families, and of course, Marjorie Cassel Hitchcock and Claude N. Hitchcock, my mother, Katherine Hitchcock Bailey, and my father, Peter O'Brien Bailey, who despite their own Roads of Challenges, answered the Call to Adventure and launched my Heroic Journey.

Peter Hitchcock Bailey, peter.bailey@proutyproject.com

About the Author

Peter Bailey greets the sunrise every day with gratitude and a strong cup of black coffee. He looks for shapes in clouds, often quotes *Lonesome Dove* and *Sherlock Holmes*, and muses about fly-fishing. He is a multifaceted experiential educator and facilitator who has delivered forty years of leadership-based adventure and innovative programs to executives and management teams around the world. He has traveled, worked, and lived in over fifty countries. Minnesota is home for his family and furry critters, and he still wonders if he shouldn't be taller.